THE END OF
THE ROMAN WORLD

The End of
the Roman World

By

STEWART PEROWNE, 1901

"*L'empire, je l'avoue, est encor quelque chose,
Mais nous ne sommes plus au temps de Théodose.*"
Corneille, *Attila*, II, 189–90.

"Every generation has an innate sympathy
with some epoch of the past wherein it seems
to find itself foreshadowed."
Bernard Berenson, Preface to first edition
of *Venetian Painters*, 1894.

THOMAS Y. CROWELL COMPANY
Established 1834
New York

First published in the United States of America in 1967

Copyright © 1966 by Stewart Perowne

Printed in Great Britain

Library of Congress Catalog Card No. 67-10944

First Printing

To
David and Patricia

TEXT ACKNOWLEDGEMENTS

I should like to thank the following publishers for giving me their permission to quote:

Librairie Bloud et Gay for a quotation from *Historie de l'Eglise* by J.-R. Palanque.

Westminster Press for quotations from *St Augustine of Hippo: Life and Controversies* by Gerald Bonner.

Chapman and Hall Ltd for a quotation from Bernard Berenson's *The Arch of Constantine.*

The Loeb Classical Library for quotations from their editions of the *Augustan History, Ausonius* and *Ammianus.*

PREFACE

This book is not as presumptuous as its title might suggest. It would be rash indeed to attempt to retell the story which has been told so grandly by Gibbon, in later years with more accuracy by Hodgkin, by Dill, by the Cambridge Medieval Historians and in our own day by Professor A. H. M. Jones. The object of this study is modest: it is simply to examine to what extent and in what manner the spirit of Rome was perpetuated in Church and State. Even so it may be thought arrogant to attempt it: but I felt it would be cowardly not to attempt it. Having over the last decade written four books in which I have endeavoured to trace the spiritual evolution of the Roman world, not to have at least tried to carry the story down to the end of the fifth century would, I thought, have been rather craven. So here is the final essay in the series.

I am indebted to many for much help. The Director of the British School at Rome generously allowed me to write the greater part of the book there. The Master and Fellows of Corpus Christi College, Cambridge, shewed me a similar indulgence. I am very grateful to the Directors of the National Museums in Damascus, Istanbul and Tunis for so readily supplying me with photographs, and to the International Cultural Centre at Tunis for gracious hospitality. The Revd Joseph Crehan, S.J., has once again given me of his time and scholarship, and once again I thank him truly. Mr Peter Llewellyn, of Jesus College, Oxford, kindly read much of the typescript and offered valuable advice. Last, and specially, I thank Mr Atis Antonovics of Pembroke College, Oxford, for his constant help, guidance and encouragement.

S. P.
London
England
1966

CONTENTS

MAPS

ILLUSTRATIONS
(between pp. 92-3)

xi

ACKNOWLEDGEMENTS

1 National Museum of Damascus
2 Bardo Museum, Tunis
3 Somerset County Museum, Taunton
4 Anderson
5 British Museum
6 National Archaeological Museum, Istanbul
7 Alinari
8 Archivo Fotografico, Vatican Museums, Rome
9 Mansell Collection
10 Victoria and Albert Museum: Crown copyright
11 Aerofilms and Aero Pictorial Ltd
12 Carthage Museum
13 W. J. White, Hinton St Mary
14 Marcel Bovis, Paris
15 Biblioteca Ambrosiana, Milan; photograph by Scansoni Walter
16 Copyright the Frick Collection, New York
17 Ann Munchow, Aachen

INTRODUCTION

"After the fatigue of walking over the immense circuit of the city, we used often to stop at the Baths of Diocletian; sometimes we even climbed upon the vaulted roof of that once magnificent building, for nowhere is there a healthier air, a wider prospect, or more silence and desirable solitude. There we did not talk of business nor of private or public affairs on which we had shed tears enough. As we walked over the walls of the shattered city or sat there, the fragments of the ruins were under our very eyes. Our conversation turned on history, which we appeared to have divided up between us in such a fashion that in modern history you, in ancient history I, seemed to be more expert; and *ancient* were called those events which took place before the name of Christ was celebrated in Rome, and adored by the Roman emperors, *modern*, however, the events from that time to the present."

Thus does Petrarch write to his friend Giovanni Colonna in November, 1341.[1] In April of that year Petrarch had paid his second visit to Rome in order to be crowned on the Capitol as poet laureate. On his former visit, four years earlier, he had been so overwhelmed by the impression of greatness made desolate that he had been unable to pay it any tribute except that of silence; but on this second visit he has become articulate once more. For the English reader, the passage cited above (the original is in Latin) has overtones which echo Gibbon "musing on the Capitol, while the bare-footed fryars were chanting their litanies in the temple of Jupiter", or of Shelley dreaming in the baths of Caracalla, and well it may; for we have here, in Petrarch's letter of 1341, the first evidence of an interest in pagan Rome rather than Christian Rome, the city which Petrarch had loved ever since his childhood, "the city which has no peer, nor ever can have". For the first time, both for Petrarch and for those who came after him, the boundary is erected between ancient history and modern history. Henceforth the "dark" ages will be not those which preceded the birth of Christ, but those which succeeded the fall of Rome. "By setting up the 'decline of the Empire' as a dividing point

[1] Th. Mommsen, *Medieval and Renaissance Studies*, Cornell University Press, 1959, p. 115.

xiii

and passing over the traditional marks either of the foundation of the Empire or of the birth of Christ, Petrarch introduced a new chronological demarcation in history."[1] A century later we find the great Italian humanist Flavio Biondo actually entitling his history *Decades historiarum ab inclinatione imperii*, "from the decline of the empire", a chronicle of the period from 410, the year in which Alaric sacked Rome, down to the year 1440, for which reason it is generally reckoned that the new method of historical division, the use of the year 410 as a cardinal date, derives from the mid-fifteenth century. But it is clear that Petrarch viewed history in this way a hundred years earlier.

Once established, the division stuck. The year 410 became to Roman history what 1066 was to be for English history, the Great Divide. What preceded it was Rome, what came after decay. In the sixteenth century this feeling of loss, of treasure ravished and forgotten, found its way into the thoughts of the poets. Joachim du Bellay gave it its most poignant expression in his *Antiquités de Rome*. Of this famous sonnet-sequence the best known is No. 3, which so moved our own Edmund Spenser that he translated it into English:

> *Thou stranger, which for Rome in Rome here seekest*
> *And nought of Rome in Rome perceiv'st at all,*
> *Then some olde walls, olde arches, which thou seest*
> *Olde Palaces, is that which Rome men call.*
> *Beholde what wrecke, what ruine, and what wast,*
> *And how that she, which with her mighty powre*
> *Tam'd all the world, hath tam'd herself at last;*
> *The pray of time, which all things doth devowre!*
> *Rome now of Rome is th'only funerall,*
> *And onely Rome of Rome hath victorie,*
> *Ne ought save Tyber hasting to his fall*
> *Remains of all. O World's inconstancie!*
> *That which is firme doth flit and fall away*
> *And that is flitting doth abide and stay.*

Here, lamentation has supplanted history, and the romantic ecstasy which was to possess so many Rome-fanciers in succeeding ages is already claiming its adepts.

It is this Rome "before the Fall" that caught the imagination of Shakespeare. His choice of plots was, it is true, limited by the fact that Plutarch, from whom, through Amyot and North,

---

[1] Mommsen, *op. cit.*

he acquired them, lived in the hey-day, the golden noon of the empire. But from his treatment of them, even of a republican Coriolanus, it is clear that it was "the imperial theme" that enthralled him. Even in *Hamlet*, amid the myths and mists of the cold north, Shakespeare recalls "the most high and palmy state of Rome". It was the same with Ben Jonson, both of whose tragedies, *Catiline* and *Sejanus*, are drawn from Roman sources.

Most significant of all, because so close a parallel with Petrarch, is Milton. Like Petrarch, Milton was a man of deep religious conviction, to whom if for anyone the age of darkness is the period between "man's first disobedience" and his redemption. And yet, in the proem to Book IV of *Paradise Regained*, imperial Rome is held out by the Tempter in lines of incomparable majesty as the most glittering prize the world has to offer: the sectary is lost in the poet, and for a while at least the Eternal City is for him too a city made by Roman hands:

> *The City which thou seest no other deem*
> *Than great and glorious* Rome, *Queen of the Earth*
> *So far renown'd, and with the spoils enricht*
> *Of Nations; there the Capitol thou seest*
> *Above the rest lifting his stately head*
> *On the* Tarpeian *rock, her Cittadel*
> *Impregnable, and there Mount* Palatine
> *The Imperial Palace, compass huge, and high*
> *The Structure, skill of noblest Architects,*
> *With gilded battlements conspicuous far,*
> *Turrets and Terrases, and glittering Spires.*
> *Many a fair Edifice besides, more like*
> *Houses of Gods (so well I have dispos'd*
> *My Aerie Microscope) thou may'st behold*
> *Outside and inside both, pillars and roofs*
> *Carv'd work, the hand of fam'd Artificers*
> *In* Cedar, Marble, Ivory *or Gold.*
> *Thence to the gates cast round thine eye, and see*
> *What conflux issuing forth, or entring in,*
> *Pretors, Proconsuls to thir Provinces*
> *Hasting or on return, in robes of State;*
> *Lictors and rods the ensigns of thir power,*
> *Legions and Cohorts, turmes of horse and wings:*
> *Or Embassies from Regions far remote*
> *In various habits on the* Appian *road,*
> *Or on the* Aemilian, *some from farthest South,*

Syene, *and where the shadow both way falls,*
Meroe Nilotic *Isle, and more to West,*
The Realm of Bocchus *to the* Black-moor *Sea;*
From the Asian *Kings and* Parthian *among these,*
From India *and the golden* Chersoness
And utmost Indian *Isle* Taprobane,
Dusk faces with white silken Turbants wreath'd:
From Gallia, Gades, *and the* British *West,*
Germans *and* Scythians, *and* Sarmatians *North*
Beyond Danubius *to the* Tauric *Pool.*
All Nations now to Rome *obedience pay,*
To Rome's *great Emperour, whose wide domain*
In ample Territory, wealth and power,
Civility of Manners, Arts, and Arms,
And long Renown thou justly may'st prefer
Before the Parthian; these two Thrones except,
The rest are barbarous, and scarce worth the fight,
Shar'd among petty Kings too far remov'd.

The pathos, and to some extent the point, of these lines lie out-side them. As a young man Milton had visited Rome, where he was caressed by its politest society, admired for his manners, his looks and his scholarship. The Forum was then what it was in Du Bellay's days, and was to remain for another two centuries, the *campo vaccino,* the cow-pasture. And yet, old, blind and neglected, Milton, with his poet's radar eye, could bring the imperial original back to three-dimensioned life as no modern device of photography or lighting could ever do.

For the age of Milton, as for Milton himself, imperial Rome was a tremendous, dominating fact. The very name of Rome seemed to toll like a knell across the wastes of time. Never had man before or since raised so lofty a creation; and yet it was fallen, for ever fallen. The fact was accepted: but in a rational age reasons must be found for it.

The stages through which the debate has passed have been lucidly summarized by Momigliano.[1] The two questions to which an answer, or answers, have to be found are: WHY did the Roman empire come to an end, and WHEN did the Roman empire come to an end? Because ever since the fourteenth century men had been profoundly convinced that the civiliza-tion of the age preceding their own was radically different from

---

[1] *The Conflict between Paganism and Christianity in the Fourth Century: Essays edited by Arnaldo Momigliano,* Oxford 1963: Introduction.

the world of classical Rome. "The greatest of the Latin poets of the eleventh century, Hildebert of Lavardin, was under no illusion about the state of Rome: '*Par tibi, Roma, nihil, cum sis prope tota ruina*'."[1]

Biondo had a precise answer to both questions. The Roman empire was overthrown from without, by the Goths, the barbarians, in the year 410. Biondo had few followers. For Machiavelli, in the sixteenth century, it was Rome's faulty constitution that was the solvent. In 1734 Montesquieu published his *Considérations sur la grandeur et la décadence des Romains*. Gibbon, heir to a long tradition, "conceived the first thought" of his history just thirty years later. There is in Montesquieu a certain bias against the Christians, although it was to the power of the army and excessive luxury that he chiefly attributed the great disaster. Voltaire sustains the anti-Christian note, which in Gibbon becomes a diapason. Gibbon justly identified Christianity as the chief agent of *change* in Roman society; but he attributed the decadence of that society to the same source.

During the nineteenth century, when historical research was largely in the hands of Germans, it became fashionable to attribute the downfall of Rome to German invasions. "The most coherent alternative view was elaborated by Marx and his followers when they claimed that the Roman empire fell because its social structure, founded as it was on slavery, was replaced by the feudal economic system."[2]

Thus confusingly complex had the problem become by the end of the nineteenth century. During the past fifty years painstaking research by the scholars of many countries has made it a good deal more complicated. In brief, three new factors have been taken into account. The first is Byzantium. Gibbon, it is true, carries his story down to the year 1483, when the Turks captured Constantinople, and the Byzantine era came to an end; but for Gibbon the whole millennium of Byzantine existence was only a shabby aftermath of the glories of Rome. Nowadays we take a very different view: Byzantium is regarded as the hearth of one of the world's greatest civilizations, and as the cradle of some of its greatest arts. Secondly, a larger share in the transformation from Rome to the Middle Ages is now allotted to tribes who were not German at all, but Slavs, or Huns: it was their relentless pressure that goaded the

[1] *Ibid.* "Rome, there is nothing like thee, although thou art almost wholly ruined."

[2] Momigliano, *op. cit.*

B

Germanic tribes into conflict with Rome. Thirdly, there are those who claim that there was little break in the ordinary routines of life after the coming of the outlanders, and that it was only the advent of the Arabs in the seventh century that broke up the organic unity of the Mediterranean – and even the Arabs, having no urban civilization of their own, adopted the civilization they found ready to hand, just as the northern intruders had done before them. Rostovtzeff saw the decline of town life as fatal; but he also realized that although much had perished, specially in the arts, much lived on. "Though that world grew old, it never died and it never disappeared: it lives on in us, as the groundwork of our thought, our attitude to religion, our art, our social and political institutions and even our material civilization."[1] And now to gather up all the threads, as it were, comes the Cyclopean work of Jones.[2] This its author modestly calls "a social, economic and administrative survey", but it is in fact a thesaurus of all that it is known of the period, with the exception of the domain of the arts. Of these Professor Jones does not treat, but, as we shall see, this particular field has been fruitfully cultivated by others.

From the foregoing prismatic array, one shaft of light illuminates the entire scene: it is that which throws into relief a simple fact against a complex background, namely that no one reason either external or internal accounts for the decline of Rome.

The corollary to that theorem is that no one date does either. Biondo chose 410, but there are plenty more to choose from. It may be helpful to tabulate them, like this:

312   Battle of Milvian Bridge: Constantine master of Rome.
330   Constantinople, "New Rome", inaugurated.
394   Battle of river Frigidus: Theodosius defeats last pagan pretender.
476   Romulus Augustulus, last "Roman" emperor, deposed.
565   Death of Justinian.
800   Coronation of Charlemagne.
1453   Fall of Constantinople to Ottoman Turks.
1806   Napoleon compels Francis II to declare ended the Holy Roman Empire.

The "When?" is no less complicated than the "Why?"

[1] *A History of the Ancient World*, Rome, *ad fin.*
[2] *The Later Roman Empire*, 284–602, by A. H. M. Jones, Blackwell, 1964.

The aim of the present study is modest. It seeks only to review the various reasons given for the decline of Rome, to examine their validity, and to give some estimate of how much Rome lived on in the succeeding ages. It is this third and last aim which is the most arresting and the most important. Nowadays we have ceased to think of history as a tabular record, in which "age" follows "age", and dynasty dynasty, the beginnings and endings of which are marked by the boundary-stones of dates. We prefer to regard time as "an ever-rolling stream", of which the volume may vary from one epoch to another, but which remains one and indivisible. What came after Rome, therefore, was (as Rostovtzeff knew) the product of Rome itself; and so our own age is, at long remove, its progeny and heir.

First, some attempt will be made to assess the general state of society in the fourth and fifth centuries, its armed force, its government, its art, its religion. Then, a brief account of the external forces at work, from Persia to Germany, to the detriment of the Roman peace, will be given. Finally, something will be said of those who were striving, and striving successfully, to build a new world on the débris of the old.

PART ONE

CHAPTER I

ROMAN TWILIGHT

Every day has two twilights; but it is the second, the dusk that precedes the dark, that has always caught the imagination of mankind, because it is the dark that is the symbol of death to which all men are consigned. So it is with states. How many could recall the origins of the empires of, say, Assyria, Russia or Turkey, how few not know at least the outlines of their eclipse? To this rule Rome is no exception; only the end of Rome is far more baffling to comprehend. Some of the reasons for this lack of precision, for this unfocused outline as it were, have been suggested in the Introduction. But there are others.

Unlike Assyria or Russia, neither of which, any more than the Ottoman or Chinese empires, made any intimate contribution to our own civilization, Rome made a larger contribution than any other source, a contribution which still endures. In law, in administration, in the urban organization of our lives, behind the realities of to-day, we often discern a Roman phantom. Then, too, the actual Romans, in their habit as they lived, seem so familiar to us. Roman portrait sculpture, at its best, was among the finest the world has ever seen: it was not to be equalled until the days of the early Renaissance, a thousand years later.[1] Many of these Romans look like Englishmen in togas, a resemblance much helped by the custom of representing Englishmen in marble as Romans in togas.[2] Many a Roman emperor looks hauntingly like some English worthy of the eighteenth or nineteenth century, and so we are apt to transfer back to them the ideas and standards of our own countrymen. (This happens less often with the ladies, because the hair-styles of Roman matrons, although they were as fantastic as those of Englishwomen, were ridiculous in a noticeably different way.) Another beguiling error arises from the

---

[1] Berenson agreed with this view.

[2] The last memorial of a statesman so garbed is probably that by Carew of Huskisson in Chichester Cathedral. He was the first statesman to be run over by a locomotive, at the opening of the Liverpool and Manchester Railway in 1830.

fact that the Romans, like the English, were great letter-writers. Cicero in the last days of the Republic, Pliny in the second century A.D., even Symmachus in the fourth, wrote letters which might persuade us that their lives and thoughts were far more like our own than they actually were.

When we examine such literature as survives from the fourth century, and even more when we survey its art, we realize not only that the Romans of that age were far different from those of two centuries earlier but also that they are even more different from our own selves.

The very term "fourth century" is misleading. That is how we reckon it, and it makes the age sound very "early", almost primitive. To the Romans of the day, on the other hand, as indeed to everyone else, it was not the fourth century at all, it was the eleventh. More than a century earlier, in what by our reckoning was the year 257, Rome had celebrated its millennium. Its citizens were conscious of being the children of a very glorious, very ancient city. This attitude is of cardinal importance. The Eternal City – that was what men called Rome. The phrase is first known to have been used by the poet Tibullus, who died in 19 B.C.[1] But within the century it had become common parlance, and the emperors placed the word "eternity" on their coins. By the time of which we are treating, that is some two hundred years later, the words Eternal City were no more than a synonym, almost a technical term, for Rome.[2] This is all the more remarkable because Rome was no longer the seat of government, and had not been for many years. The first danger signal to Rome's inviolable permanence had been raised in the year 270, for it was then that the emperor Aurelian had decided that the city must once again be girt with defensive walls. No wall had been built around Rome since the dread days of the Gaulish invasion in the fourth century B.C. For more than five hundred years the defence of Rome had lain on her frontiers, and it was there in dim and distant lands that walls were built, including two in our own country. Suddenly, in the days of Aurelian, the frontier receded from the Tyne to the Tiber – as dramatic a warning as could be devised of what lay in store for civilization. In fact, Rome itself was to be spared for another one hundred and thirty

[1] II. v. 23: *"Romulus aeternae nondum formaverat urbis Moenia"*: "Romulus had not yet traced the walls of the Eternal City."

[2] Ammianus Marcellinus, the last historian of Rome to write in Latin, at the very end of the fourth century, regularly so describes the city. Cf. p. 65.

years; but other provinces of the empire knew invasion, and Athens itself was sacked by barbarians in the year 292. The story of these inroads, involved and complicated as it is, must be reserved for a later chapter: here it is only desired to make the point that because of them, Rome was no longer the strategic or even the administrative capital of the empire. At the end of the third century Diocletian had ruled from Nicomedia, on the Asian shore opposite Byzantium. Trier, Milan, Sardica in Dacia, and after 330 Constantinople – all these became imperial residences and administrative centres. Diocletian is believed to have visited Rome only once, to commemorate the twentieth year of his reign.[1] Later emperors would be no more assiduous. Constantine, during the last thirteen years of his reign, visited Rome once only, like Diocletian for his *vicennalia*. But the very fact that it was in Rome, and not elsewhere, that these rulers felt bound to celebrate this solemn anniversary is evidence of the prestige and esteem which the City still enjoyed. Even when, in 330, Constantinople was inaugurated, it was designated only the *second* Rome. It did not originally share, and even later never juridically supplanted, the primacy of Rome in either ecclesiastical or civil affairs. Its principal officer was a proconsul, not a prefect as in Rome. It had no quaestors, praetors or tribunes of the people – the time-honoured executives of Rome. It had a senate, it is true, but its members were designated only *clari*, not *clarissimi* as the Roman senators were. Constantinople was in theory and in fact simply one, admittedly the most magnificent, of the imperial residences. It must be remembered that Constantine himself endowed Rome with baths,[2] with magnificent churches, and that he completed the basilica which still bears his name, one of the most imposing audience chambers of all antiquity. In the year 357 Constantius, the son of Constantine, paid a visit to Rome, of which Ammianus gives us a detailed account.[3]

"As he was approaching the city, his calm gaze dwelt upon the courtesies offered by the senate, and so many august countenances, the very images of aristocratic ancestry. Cineas, the envoy of Pyrrhus[4], had thought that the senate was 'an

---

[1] Jones, p. 40. The Latin word for this celebration is *vicennalia*.

[2] The horse tamers now on the Quirinal flanked the entrance to Constantine's Baths.

[3] XVI, x.

[4] King of Epirus, invaded Italy, 280 B.C. At first successful in battle, he was in the end forced to return owing to his numerous losses. Hence "Pyrrhic victory".

assembly of kings'; but to the emperor they appeared as the sanctuary of the entire world. Turning his eyes from them to the populace, he was amazed at the numbers in which every type of mankind had flocked from all over the world to Rome." Ammianus then describes the body-guard with a soldier's eye for detail, the mail-clad infantrymen, and the masked cuirassiers, clad wholly in iron, who looked more like statues polished by Praxiteles than real man.[1] The imperial standards were made of purple webs, contrived to look like dragons, which hissed and waved their tails in the wind – an indication of how oriental the imperial image was becoming, as was also the absolute impassivity with which the emperor responded, or failed to respond, to the plaudits of the crowds. "Then he entered Rome, the very hearth and home of empire and of all virtue; and when he had come to the Rostra, the most outstanding forum of ancient power, he was amazed. Wherever he looked, he was overcome by the sheer density of miraculous creations. He addressed the nobility in the senate-house, and the people from the tribunal He was then taken up to the palace,[2] with many deferential attentions, and at last enjoyed what he had for so long looked forward to. He often provided equestrian games, and took pleasure in the back-chat of the plebs, because, while they were conscious of their traditional freedom, they never went too far. He, also, kept the right balance. In other cities the contests would be ended at his sole discretion, but not here: he left them to be brought to a conclusion in the natural way of things, as they happened to go.

"He then toured the city and suburbs, enclosed within the summits of the seven hills, or on their slopes, or on the level ground below; and thought that whatever he caught sight of was the finest thing he had yet seen. There were the shrines of Tarpeian Jupiter,[3] which seemed to excel in the same way as the divine excels the human; the baths the size of provinces,

---

[1] Praxiteles did work in bronze (Pliny, *Natural History*, XXXIV, 69), but more "famously and successfully" in marble (*ibid.*, XXXVI, 20–23). The reference here, including as it does, mention of the "mask" helmets, which were of silver, seems to be to brightly polished white marble. If so, this passage is evidence in favour of the authenticity of the "Hermes of Praxiteles" at Olympia.

[2] That is the vast array of buildings on the *Palatine*, the residence of the Caesars from the days of Augustus, whence the generic term *palatium* or palace.

[3] i.e., the temples on the Capitol, including that of Jupiter Capitolinus and the Tarpeian Rock.

almost; the huge bulk of the amphitheatre,[1] reinforced with its framework of Travertine, so high that one can hardly see its top; the Pantheon[2] like a shapely city-district, vaulted over in soaring beauty; the great columns with galleries at the top, bearing the images of former emperors;[3] the temple of the city,[4] the Forum of Peace,[5] the theatre of Pompey,[6] the Odeum,[7] the Stadium[8] and all the other sights of the Eternal City. But when he came to the Forum of Trajan, which is unique in the whole world, and something which even the gods, I should say, would regard as a marvel, he stopped short in his tracks, dumbfounded, turning his attention to the gigantic complex around him, which defied description, and will never again be emulated by human enterprise. Giving up all hope of ever attempting anything like it, he said that he would, and could, only copy Trajan's horse, which stands in the middle of the court, bearing the ruler himself. Whereupon prince Ormisda, who was standing near him, and whose departure from Persia has already been related, replied with his native wit: 'First, Emperor, have a like stable built, so that the horse you propose to make can have as wide a range as the one we are looking at.' When he was asked direct what he thought of Rome, Ormisda said he took comfort in one thing only, that he had learned that even there men were mortal." In the end Constantius' contribution to the sights of Rome was a huge obelisk, brought from Egypt, and set up in the Great Circus. It was, and still is, the oldest and tallest (32·50 metres) obelisk ever to be brought to Rome. Since 1588 it has stood outside St John Lateran.

For help in forming some idea of the overwhelming impression made on a visitor by the Eternal City – and Ammianus, too, although he lived and wrote in Rome, was not a native of

[1] The Colosseum, inaugurated in A.D. 80.

[2] The work, in its present form, of Hadrian, c. A.D. 125. Its dome, 43·30 metres in circumference, is still the widest in the world.

[3] Those of Trajan and Marcus Aurelius still stand. St Peter has replaced the former, St Paul the latter.

[4] The double temple of Venus, Rome's patroness, and Rome, built by Hadrian in A.D. 135. It was the largest temple in Rome. Parts of it still stand, near the Colosseum.

[5] Built by Vespasian in A.D. 71 after the capture of Jerusalem. Vestiges of it may be seen beneath the church of SS. Cosmas and Damian.

[6] Rome's first stone-built theatre, erected in 55 B.C., The curvature of part of its enclosing wall still shows in the Via di Grotta Pinta.

[7] A concert-hall built by Domitian.

[8] Its conformation is almost exactly preserved in the Piazza Navona.

the city – the foregoing narrative has a twofold value. First, it shews how awe-inspiring the rigid Constantius found the still predominantly pagan Rome, such a contrast to Constantinople, which had never been sullied by pagan worship; and secondly, it enables us to enter into the mind and emotions of such a visitor, because with one exception, the Odeum, greater or smaller traces of all the glories catalogued by Ammianus are still to be discerned – it is still those very monuments which, after sixteen hundred years, make us of the twentieth century bow our heads before the glories of Rome.

Even so, the inventory is not complete: imperial Rome was even more grandiose and glittering than the foregoing would suggest. By great good fortune there has come down to us a document which lists the chief buildings and monuments in each of the fourteen "regions" into which Augustus had divided the city, as they stood in the days of Constantine.[1] The wealth of dignity and amenity assembled over the centuries is almost beyond the grasp of the imagination. The gilded temple of Jupiter on the Capitol, which gave Rome its mediaeval name of the golden city, reflected the rays of the rising sun across the Forum to the marble colonnades and lofty cupolas of the Palatine. In the hollow below, on either side of the Sacred Way, stood a galaxy of temples, dedicated to former emperors, to the Dioscuri, to Concord, to the goddess Vesta, the house of whose virgin votaries stood hard by. There were triumphal arches, of which three[2] still stand, to expound to us the victories of those whom they commemorate, two of them warriors in our own land.

On either side of the Forum there stood a splendid basilica, that on the north founded by a member of the Aemilian family in 179 B.C., balanced by that of Julius Caesar on the south. To the north-west of the Aemilian basilica and the adjacent senate-house there stretched the magnificent sequence of the imperial forums, spacious and unencumbered, in calculated contrast to the crowded opulence of the original Forum Romanum, the heart of Rome.

---

[1] The *Notitia Dignitatum*. See Jones, p. 689, and his Appendix II.

[2] The arch of *Titus* was erected by the senate after his death to celebrate his capture of Jerusalem. The arch of *Septimius Severus* erected in 203 for his tenth anniversary depicts scenes from his eastern campaigns. It was originally surmounted by a bronze quadriga. Septimius Severus died at York. The arch of *Constantine* was placed near the Colosseum in 315 by the senate to commemorate his victory at the Milvian Bridge which made him master of Rome, the climax of a march which had started at York, where his troops had hailed him as emperor.

This was the great quadrilateral of the city's splendour, bounded by the Capitol, the Palatine, the Colosseum and the imperial forums, with the Forum Romanum inside it; but every quarter of the city was embellished with monuments of unsurpassed elegance. To this day we can admire the remains of the portico erected by Livia, the wife of Augustus, near the theatre of Marcellus, we can peruse the sculptured message of his own altar of peace, now re-erected near the terraced rotunda of his mausoleum. Across the river is the equally imposing tomb of Hadrian. We can even grope our way through the dank and eerie chambers of Nero's Golden House. In the museums of Rome, as in some of its surviving buildings, we can be charmed by paintings of the Roman countryside, and stucco reliefs of unrivalled delicacy. Eight bridges spanned the Tiber, and led to the gardens and pleasure grounds of the Janiculum, below which lay the circus of Caligula, whence originally rose the obelisk which now stands before St Peter's. No less than thirteen obelisks were scattered through the city, eight of them transported from Egypt, and five manufactured in Rome itself. Fourteen aqueducts supplied innumerable fountains as well as the artificial lakes and baths of the city. More than four thousand statues of gods and men adorned its temples, libraries and colonnades. There are said to have been 1,797 private houses and 46,602 *insulae* – islands, or apartment blocks. From these figures many attempts have been made to deduce the number of the urban population. The most commendable seems to be that of Carcopino,[1] who would place the total of Rome's inhabitants at not less than 1,200,000.

So splendid and august a city, venerated as the eternal summit and centre of the universe, thronged by such a concentration of citizens, seems ideally equipped to assume, or to retain, the primacy of the civilized world, and to be the abode par excellence of men of light and leading in the realms of politics, learning, commerce and the arts. In fact, the Rome of the fourth century, despite all the adulation bestowed upon it, was nothing of the sort.

Its status is concisely defined by Professor Jones:[2]

"Rome was already in Diocletian's day an anachronism. It had ceased to be the capital of the empire in any but a formal sense, and it never became so again. As an administrative centre, Rome was under the later empire of no greater importance

---

[1] *La Vie Quotidienne à Rome*, by Jérôme Carcopino, pp. 34 *seq.*
[2] p. 687.

than a dozen other cities which were capitals of dioceses.[1]
It had never possessed any industry which served a wider
public than its own citizens, and the establishment of an
imperial clothing factory cannot have greatly enhanced its
economic importance. It had never been a centre of commerce.
Its survival as a large and prosperous city was due to its antique
political prerogatives and to the growth of its new spiritual
supremacy."

Of the citizenry it is not easy to form any precise or vivid
picture. The supreme magistrate was the *praefectus urbi*, the
City Prefect, an office which went back to the days of Augustus,
and was usually held, for little more than a year, by members of
the old aristocracy. The prefect was president of the senate,
judge of the senators themselves and judge of appeal in all
causes within a hundred miles of Rome. He was also responsible for the public services of the city. Attached to him,
though appointed by the emperor, were a number of minor
officials. There was a curator of aqueducts, another of the banks
and bed of the Tiber and the sewers.[2] Other officers were responsible for public buildings, for the innumerable statues,
for the storehouses of oil and wine, for the harbours at Ostia
and Portus, for the police, for the theatres and brothels, for the
corn and bread. One official had the charming title of *tribunus
rerum nitentium*, the tribune of the shining things, which pre-
sumably meant the precious statues and fittings of the temples,
whose gilded tiles and capitals must have been a continual
temptation to the impoverished.

Besides all these, the ancient magistrates, the consuls, the
quaestors and the praetors were still appointed from the ranks
of the senate, though their chief function was now to provide
"games" whereat gladiators would be set to fight each other to
the death, or opposed to rare and beautiful beasts collected, at
vast expense, from all over the empire. There were four schools
for gladiators in the city. Symmachus, one of the last and the
best of the pagans, who was City Prefect towards the end of the
fourth century, decided in the year 393 to vary the excitement of
the contests by importing a company of Saxons, twenty-nine in

[1] Major administrative divisions of the empire as reorganized by Diocletian.

[2] It is a strange fact that the Romans, with all their engineering skill
and enterprise, never succeeded in mastering the Tiber, which repeatedly
caused disastrous floods. In fact, it was only in the 'seventies of the last
century, largely at the instance of Garibaldi, that the river was adequately
embanked.

number, from the far north, an enterprise which must have cost him a pretty penny. But, as he complains in a letter to his brother, these unco-operative brutes, rather than be butchered to make a Roman holiday, strangled themselves in their cells before the great day dawned. For Symmachus, normally a kind-hearted man, this is just a dirty barbarian trick.[1] It is hard to tell from such a letter as this just how rotten senatorial society really was. If we are to believe Ammianus, it was rotten to the core; but his famous denunciation of the manners and morals of "high society" in the Rome of his day has a familiar whine, to anyone acquainted with the analogous denunciations of Isaiah, Juvenal or Hogarth. Indeed, the passage[2] in which he castigates the off-hand behaviour of an aristocratic patron to his client is so like Dr Johnson's famous letter to Lord Chesterfield that it is hard to believe that it was not the model for it. Ammianus tells us in the same passage that "not very long ago, when there was fear of a food shortage, foreigners were turned out of the city neck and crop, and those who practised the liberal arts – there were only a few – were packed off without time to breathe; yet the impresarios of the mimes, and those who pretended to be such, were allowed to stay, together with three thousand dancing-girls, as many dancing-masters and their choruses, without any questions being asked". From which the inference is that Ammianus, being an Antiochene, was one of the "foreigners" expelled. He refers to the professors of the liberal arts as being few. But some there still were, with official salaries attached. They taught rhetoric, grammar, philosophy and law. Symmachus once had occasion to complain to the praetorian prefect of Italy that a professor's salary had been wrongly withheld. Students had to be duly registered, and could be beaten and sent home for unsatisfactory conduct. None was allowed to stay after the age of twenty.[3]

No less violent than the pagan Ammianus is the Christian Jerome. As a young man he, too, had known Roman society. At the time when he wrote the letters in which he denounces it, he was living an ascetic life in Bethlehem. He, too, we feel, is painting too lurid a picture. His contemporary Macrobius, a pagan of the old school, gives a far more attractive description of decent "old" Roman society. He wrote a charming work called *Saturnalia*, a title which might mislead modern readers, because the assembly it describes is the complete reverse of

[1] Letters, II, 46.   [2] XIV, 6, 12.   [3] Jones, p. 707.

what the word nowadays implies. It shews the leading pagan aristocrats, Symmachus, Albinus, Flavianus and Praetextatus, spending together the days of the Saturnalia, which corresponded to our Christmas festivities. In the mornings they held discussions on literary or antiquarian subjects; in the evenings, over dinner, the talk was lighter and gayer. But, in contrast to the vulgar Belshazzars of the ultra-rich, the food and drink are noteworthy for their moderation, and there was naturally no cabaret show at such a gathering. In fact, Macrobius actually claims that his generation is more decent than their ancestors.[1]

Of the populace it is easy to form a more consistent and less favourable judgement. Unlike their betters, they had not even the limited responsibilities of the senatorial *cursus honorum*. They gave no games, they held no chairs, they were not even civil servants. They had no political existence at all. Drawn from every realm of the empire, they were parasites upon the body politic. One of the privileges that Rome enjoyed was free food. The number of those entitled to it had decreased over the years, but even in the middle of the fifth century there were no less than 120,000 ration-card holders. Ration-cards could change hands by inheritance or sale: they were a valuable property. The daily bread ration in the latter half of the fourth century was six half-pound loaves, produced from corn levied in Africa, ground by water-mills and baked in 274 public bakeries. There was a free issue of oil, and for 150 days a year of pork as well, at the rate of five pounds a month. Wine was not provided free, but at very low prices. The state had more wine on its hands than it could dispose of, and sometimes made payments by means of it. Any diminution of the issue of food or wine might cause a riot among the pampered plebs.[2] The slaughter of the amphitheatre and the rivalries of the race-course were its chief preoccupations.

Such in brief outline was the Eternal City in the fourth century. A strong mosaic it was of good and bad, of old and new. There was much in it to blame. It was spoiled, enfeebled; above all, it was in complete bondage to its past. But it was beautiful and it was tough. It commanded, and would, despite all the vicissitudes of invasion and spoliation, continue to command, the almost universal veneration of mankind,

---

[1] *Sat.*, II, i, 6, and Dill, *Roman Society in the Last Century of the Western Empire*, pp. 131, 210. See also p. 117 below.

[2] Cf. Amm., XIV, 6, i; XIV. 7, 5.

Roman and barbarian, pagan and Christian alike. And then, when the din of battle and the cries of despair were hushed, a new Rome would arise, to the melody of psalms and the sound of hymns.

It is to the tracing of that evolution that the following chapters will be devoted. And first we must outline the political and administrative state of the empire as it was when Constantine was its first Christian master.

CHAPTER II

CHANGE AND DECAY

Despite the dazzling vision which the Eternal City presented to the eyes of mankind in the fourth century, some shrewder spirits realized that all was not well within. Ammianus, for instance, was able to view affairs with the semi-detachment of one born in the Greek east. He admits that Rome is now "on the threshold of old age, and often conquering simply by its name alone, coming to a quieter period of life".[1] And in the same passage, while lauding the "white hair of the senators", he concedes that all the democratic assemblies of the republic have long been silent. This sense of decline was not born with the fourth century: it had been felt more than a century before. Dio Cassius – again a provincial, a Bythinian – was a talented civil servant who twice held the consulship, once in 229 as the colleague of an emperor. At the beginning of the third century he wrote a history of Rome, including the Rome of his own age, of which an epitome has survived. Summing up the great age of the Antonines, which ended with the death of Marcus Aurelius in the year 186, he writes: "our history now descends from a kingdom of gold to one of iron and rust, as the affairs of the Romans then did".[2] This judgement of Dio's was not only perceptive but prophetic; because the next half century saw the empire rent by anarchy, and a spate of pretenders setting up rebellious and dissident régimes in Africa, Asia, Gaul and Britain. But for the advent of a sequence of brave and resourceful men, natives, nearly all of them, of Illyria, the Roman dominion might well have dissolved in the third century, instead of living on into the fourth and beyond it, with a loss to future generations which it is impossible to calculate.

The decay was finally arrested and unity restored by Diocletian. This remarkable man completely reorganized the administrative structure of the empire. He ruled for twenty-one years, from 284 to 305, and then retired to his homeland of Illyria, where he built for himself at what is now Split a

[1] XIV, 6, 3.
[2] Book LXXII, *ad fin.*

fortress-palace, of which the remains still excite our admiration.[1]

As remarked above, Diocletian's reforms did, at least, postpone the collapse of the empire, they may even have decided the general pattern which its evolution would ultimately assume; but they did, also, beyond question sow the seeds of much of the internal maladies which, combined with pressure from without, afflicted the ageing state. They were extremely complicated; but since some grasp of them is essential to the comprehension of future events, an effort will be made to set them out as simply as possible.

1. *The emperor becomes an absolute monarch.* The monarchical principle had been inherent in what we call the empire ever since the days of Augustus, specially in the east, where divinity had hedged kings from time immemorial; but in theory the head of the state was a *princeps*, a chief among equals. The senate for long retained certain prerogatives, such as the minting of copper coins (gold and silver being reserved to the *princeps*), and the appointment of governors to the peaceful provinces at a distance from the frontiers. The best emperors made a point of shewing deference to the senate, rising to greet senators, and attending their meetings when in Rome. They were most anxious, in fact, to clothe the body politic, as it actually existed, in what Edmund Burke calls "the decent draperies" of life.

In the third century the scene begins to change. Emperors born in the provinces, some not even of Latin blood, were resented by the senate, and in their turn tended more and more to undermine what was left of its authority, to rely more and more on the army and on their own nominees, from the equestrian, or second, rank of society. Gallienus finally forbade senators to hold any military command.[2] Diocletian, looking back over a generation of competitive chaos, was determined that henceforth there should be no more equivocation, and that the head of the state should be its sole and unquestioned sovereign.

As his model he took his rival and neighbour, Persia. He wore silk robes of state, embroidered with gold and studded with gems: he allowed himself to be addressed as lord and "adored"

---

[1] In the year 1754 Robert Adam visited Split, or Spalato as it was then called. It was from the palace that he obtained his ideas for the Adelphi, which itself influenced Nash's designs for his famous terraces – Diocletian's bequest to London.

[2] Aurelius Victor, *Caesars*, 33.

(that is, those who were granted an audience must kiss his robe or his hand on bended knee), and to be called divine.[1] No longer would Augustus be the affable equal: he lived in numinous seclusion. His bedchamber was attended by eunuchs, another Persian importation, and one which excited universal loathing. The fact that such servants were ever considered necessary as the guardians of chastity is generally considered to damn the sexual standards of the age, and quite justly. But equally damned were the age's ideas of loyalty. It was taken as an axiom that any successful general or minister would endeavour to overthrow his master and sovereign by force or guile in favour of himself and his posterity, and for a whole century past, the annals of the empire had shewn hardly an exception to this rule of fraud and treachery. Eunuchs by their very nature could not be suspected of forming any such dynastic plans. Thus it came about that to be a eunuch could be the beginning of a successful and lucrative career, and it was with that object in view that many children were castrated, either at birth or soon after, the operators being Armenians.[2] Diocletian's assumption of open and confessed royalty may not have produced all the benefits he had hoped of it, including a new fervour of loyalty and immunity from privy conspiracy and rebellion; but it unquestionably did confer on him, and, more important, through him on the empire he ruled, an aura of divinity, which was to be a precious asset of a Rome in material decline.

2. *The Tetrarchy.* Diocletian realized almost at once that it was no longer possible for one man to govern the whole empire. He had been proclaimed Augustus at Nicomedia on 20th November, 284. Early the next year he appointed a Caesar, Maximian. That was in accordance with established practice. Ever since the end of the first century, when Vespasian appointed his sons Caesars, the title had come to be the accepted designation of the heir to the principate. But in 286 Diocletian made a wholly new departure: he appointed Maximian *Augustus*, so that there were now and henceforth not one emperor, but two emperors. With insurrections in Britain and Egypt to cope with, even two emperors were not enough, and so in 293 two Caesars were proclaimed, Constantius, father of Constantine,

---

[1] *Ibid.*, 39.

[2] See Amm., XVI, 4, 5; and Claudian, XVIII, 11, 44 *seq*. That young eunuchs also subserved the perverse lusts of both sexes undoubtedly added to the contempt in which they were held.

in the west and Galerius in the east. The Tetrarchy, or rule of four, was thus complete. The use of the word tetrarchy, and in particular the fact that there were now two Augusti, one responsible (broadly speaking) for the west, and the other for the east, has given rise to misunderstanding, and to a mistaken idea that the empire was partitioned. This is not so. Diocletian remained senior Augustus, adopting the title *Jovian* and assigning that of *Herculian* to Galerius: Jove was the king of the gods and Hercules his servant, as everybody knew – the relationship between the two Augusti could not have been made clearer. When, later on, one Augustus dwelt in Constantinople and another in Ravenna the empire was still constitutionally one. It is incorrect to speak of the emperor *of* the east or west: he was emperor *in*, not of, his region. So true is this that hundreds of years later, when the western dominion of Rome was only a memory, the emperor who reigned in Byzantium was still styled emperor of the Romans, and the people we call Byzantine were known to their Arab and Ottoman opponents as *Rum*, Roman, the word which to this day is applied to the successors of the Byzantines, namely the Orthodox Church.

The Tetrarchy survived only as long as Diocletian was there to direct it and hold it together. He thought to provide for the succession by the method of adoption, which had worked so well in the days of Trajan and Hadrian, and had given Rome its best emperors. The army thought differently: they had always been in favour of the hereditary principle, even when it meant the elevation of an Elagabalus. That is why when Constantius died in his second year as Augustus his troops at once proclaimed his son Constantine Augustus, and so started him on the course which was to lead him from York to Rome, and ultimately to the sole mastership of the empire. But Diocletian's system endured. Rightly and justly does Aurelius Victor, before mentioning any of his defects, call him *magnus vir*, a great man.

3. *The central executive.* Diocletian's only known innovation in the central direction of affairs is that he increased it fourfold to serve himself and his three colleagues. For some years past the emperors had been more out of Rome than in it, generally campaigning on the northern or eastern frontiers. It had long been a popular saying: "Where Caesar is, there Rome is."[1] This is one of the reasons why the rôle of the senate had become

[1] Herodian, *Histories*, I, vi, 5.

progressively slighter: if the emperor were absent from the capital, clearly he could not be expected to consult the conscript fathers. There thus came into being a personal staff, known as the *comitatus*. This consisted of the emperor's personal household, his bedchamber as it was known, staffed by eunuchs, together with a large subordinate staff and a bodyguard of praetorian troops, the privy council or *consistorium*, two finance ministers, various secretaries and the praetorian prefect. Of all these officers, the praetorian prefect was by far the most powerful and important. Technically the four prefects were, like their masters, a single entity; their edicts and letters were issued in their joint names, and all official communications must be addressed to all four. The praetorian prefect had originally been the officer in command of the praetorian guard, an enormously powerful subject, who on at least four occasions aspired to become emperor. The guard was disbanded in 312, but the prefects stayed on, because they now had fiscal, judicial and administrative functions which made them in effect what their Ottoman successors were to be, Grand Viziers.[1]

4. *Provincial government.* Roman provincial administration had remained almost unchanged for centuries. One reason for this was that the greater part of the empire had been acquired by the republic – a fact which is often overlooked. Britain was subdued during the first and second centuries, and Trajan added provinces beyond the Danube, the Jordan and the Euphrates, thus bringing the empire to its widest extent. Hadrian, his successor, abandoned the new eastern territories, except "Arabia" (that is, Trans-Jordan), but kept Dacia, which produced gold. Here and there what had been a tributary kingdom became a province; but compared with the enormous extent of the empire the frontier adjustments were of minor account. Sometimes a province was subdivided, as happened with both Syria and Britain, so that by Diocletian's time there were probably fifty provinces, counting Italy as one. Egypt, ever since its acquisition by Augustus after his defeat of its last

[1] It may at this point be worth noting that the resemblances between the system which Diocletian bequeathed to his successors and that of the Ottomans who inherited it from the last of them are too many to be coincidental. The Seraglio atmosphere, governmental methods, manners and often (e.g. in regard to crown lands) legislation and corruption – all these are prefigured in the Rome of the fourth century, as they survived even beyond the the end of the Ottoman empire in its former provinces. The Ottomans simply took over what they found. It lasted well.

queen, Cleopatra, in 31 B.C., had been regarded as the emperor's domain. As it was a major granary, it was vital that it should be in reliable hands, or by becoming master of Egypt a rival might blackmail his way to the purple. Vespasian had done just that. Of the fifty provinces, those on or near the frontier needed garrisons, and so they were governed by legates appointed by the emperor; the "interior" provinces, which had known peace for centuries, were governed by proconsuls elected by the senate. There was yet a third category, insignificant provinces such as Judaea in the days of Jesus of Nazareth, which were governed by an official appointed by the emperor called a procurator. Diocletian doubled the number of provinces, by drastic subdivision, and then grouped them into regional organizations called *dioceses*, each diocese being in charge of a *vicar*, answerable to the praetorian prefects. A province was governed by a *praeses*, a word which had formerly meant simply a ruler or governor without any technical signification such as it now acquired. These men were equestrians, not senators. There were practically no senatorial governorships left, except for "Asia" and "Africa", both mere fractions of what they had been, because these were the provinces that by long tradition fell to the ex-consuls to govern. Senators might also fill the new office of *corrector*, the title of the officials who were put in charge of the eight provinces into which Italy was now divided. Sicily and Achaea were also ruled by *correctores*, who were probably senators. Thus the senate did preserve a vestige of its old prerogatives in provincial government, in the two proconsular provinces and in at least some of the correctorial ones; but it was the third grade of governor, the equestrian *praeses*, who now predominated.

5. *The army*. The functions and merits of the army will be discussed in Chapter IV. Here it is only desired to indicate briefly how it was constituted and organized.[1]

As to the composition of the army it is hard to form any accurate estimate. For those brought up in an age of universal wars, when the number of armed men runs into millions, it is not always easy to scale down their ideas to the realities of antiquity. Ancient armies were never large by our standards. They might be very imposing on paper: as Jones has pointed out in a masterly analysis,[2] the combined establishment of the

---

[1] On the organization of the Roman army, see further Maj.-Gen. J. F. C. Fuller's *Julius Caesar: Man, Soldier and Tyrant*.

[2] pp. 679 *seq.*

combined armies of east and west was rather over half a million; but the army lists undoubtedly included many fictitious entries (as they had done for centuries: Hadrian had had to legislate against the practice of inserting the names of boys and old men in the registers in order to draw their pay and rations). When it came to putting an army in the field the story is very different. Zosimus,[1] quoted by Jones, tells us that the largest field force on record, that which Julian assembled for his Persian campaign, numbered 65,000 men. Other figures cited by Jones are: in 356 Constantius sent an army of 25,000 against the Alamans;[2] in 405 Stilicho had thirty regiments, plus various allies, which may have amounted to 20,000 men,[3] with which to oppose Radagaisus.[4] In the sixth century the biggest army recorded is once again one assembled for a Persian war, 52,000.[5] The great Belisarius never commanded large forces – his armies varied between 7,000 and 25,000. As for the size of the opposing armies we have almost nothing to go on. We do know that Gaiseric the Vandal took a census in the year 428/9, which shewed that he disposed of 80,000 persons, of which Jones reckons that a quarter would have been soldiers. Small field armies lasted down to quite modern times. Louis XIV, on the eve of his invasion of the Low Countries in 1672, is said to have assembled an army of 119,000 officers and men, "four times the size of any standing army in Europe since Roman days",[6] and yet at Blenheim the allies numbered 50,000 to Tallard's 54,000. At Waterloo Wellington's combined armies numbered only 67,600. The simple fact is that without modern methods of transport and production it is not possible to keep large armies in the field: they would disintegrate or starve.[7] It is only with the American Civil War, the first war to be fought with mechanical transport and mechanical production well established, that large armies as we understand them were placed in the field. In the Wilderness cam-

---

[1] II, 12 and 13.

[2] *Amm.*, XVI, 11, 2.

[3] Zosimus, V, 26. Jones does not mention the allies, but seems to have taken them into account in calculating Stilicho's strength.

[4] See p. 53 below.

[5] Procopius, *Persian War*, I, viii, 4.

[6] Vincent Cronin, *Louis XIV*, 1964, p. 192.

[7] According to Thucydides, this was true even in the Trojan war. The Achaeans' lack of success after an initial victory was, he says (I, 10, 5), "due not so much to scarcity of men as of provisions. Difficulties of supply made the invaders reduce the numbers of the army".

paign, for instance, Grant and Meade had an army of 120,000. Nevertheless, this logistical limitation, even with the malpractices noted above, does not account for the enormous discrepancy between the recorded total establishment and the small number of the field armies. The answer is that the bulk of the Roman armies were where they had always been, on the frontiers. Diocletian greatly increased the frontier garrisons, for which Zosimus praises him: "The Roman empire to its utmost limits had everywhere, by the foresight of Diocletian, been protected by towns and forts and towers, and the whole army was stationed in them. The barbarians could not get through, because they were everywhere met by troops who withstood them." [1]

What Diocletian did was to reinforce, probably to double, the frontier troops, while also preserving a mobile field force, which was developed by Constantine. There thus existed two types of soldier, the *limitanei*, or frontier troops, and the *comitatenses*, those attached to the *comitatus*, including the *protectores*, or household troops, who were theoretically available for duty on any front. In fact, many of them were dispersed in detachments in aid of the civil power – the bugbear of every commanding officer – to help maintain security and to collect the taxes. Discipline became slack, and men tended to engage in lucrative occupations while still technically soldiers. This meant that more and more recruits were necessary at a time when recruits were ever harder to come by.

The army consisted both of citizens and of barbarians. There were a few volunteers, but the majority of the citizen recruits were conscripts. The sons of soldiers and veterans were obliged to serve, and those who tried to evade their duty were liable to be rounded up by recruiting officers. Every estate or village, or group of villages, had to provide so many recruits every so many years. The levy fell wholly on the rural population. The age-limits were from nineteen to thirty-five, and the height qualification was five foot ten, reduced later to five foot seven. As soon as they were enrolled, recruits were branded, as a precaution against desertion. This fact alone shews how unpopular the service had become, and consequently how hard it now was to find enough recruits. It became progressively harder. In 397, for instance, it was proposed to enlist men from the estates of senators. The senators objected, and successfully: they were allowed to commute the levy for twenty-five *solidi* a

[1] Zosimus, II, 34.

head. By that time man-power of any kind had become so scarce that it would be ruinous to part with a single hand.[1]

Small wonder then that the army had to depend more and more on barbarian entrants. There was nothing new in principle about this. Moorish javelin-men, Osrhoenian archers, Palmyrene horsemen, these and many others had formed adjuncts of the Roman army for many years past. Often, too, Germans had crossed the Rhine and had sought service with the Romans. They made excellent troops, as Germans habitually do. Even hostages, the children and relatives of active opponents, were enlisted in the Roman army. Many of these foreigners won promotion, and to the highest ranks; so that to find a Stilicho, a Vandal, in command of a Roman army should cause us no surprise: it was simply the climax of a process that had been going on for a very long time, and had been accelerated by necessity of late years.

Many of these barbarians were now recruited from tribes settled within the empire. They were called *laeti*, which means happy, as indeed they must have been, to enjoy the amenities of civilized life after the uncertain savagery of their former existence.

The old formations, the legions, the cohorts and the wings, remained, but new cavalry units, called *vexillationes*, or detachments (from *vexilla*, banner), about 500 strong, now appear. The legions seem to have retained their traditional strength of about 6,000. A cohort numbered 600, a wing 500. Constantine increased the number of vexillations, and added a new unit of infantry, the *auxilia*.

In command of the much-increased field armies, two new officers are established, and later duplicated and more, the Master of the Foot and the Master of the Horse. The praetorian prefects retained only administrative and recruiting duties. The frontier armies were commanded by either a Count Military (*comes rei militaris*), as in Egypt, or by Dukes (*duces*) in other regions.

Federates, that is tribal units seconded under treaty, served under their own tribal leaders.

The imperial guard under Constantine was known as the *scholae*, or schools. It was under the direction not of the Military Masters, but of the Master of the Offices.

The reforms of Diocletian – and we must remember that no emperor since the great days of the Antonines had enjoyed so

[1] Jones, p. 619.

long a reign (twenty-one years) in which to realize and con-
solidate his policy – set the pattern which, as rounded out and
perfected by Constantine, was to be the constitution, as we
should now call it, of the Roman state so long as that state
should last, at any rate in its western manifestation.[1] In the
foregoing sketch (and it is no more) of the great design two
sombre facts cast deep shadows, namely the proliferation of
the bureaucracy and the alarming increase of the standing
army. To modern eyes, all too accustomed to surveying the
same phenomena, these two facts alone suggest deterioration
such as state after state has undergone in our own day. We
must now discuss why these measures were deemed to be
necessary, and more important still, what good, if any, they
achieved.

[1] Even today we use words such as vicar, diocese, count and duke, which
owe their origin to Diocletian's régime.

CHAPTER III

AFTER THREE HUNDRED YEARS

Diocletian was in the position of an heir who inherits a long-neglected property. Family disputes have wasted the capital, valuable acres have been allowed to go out of cultivation, the buildings have fallen into decay and, worst of all, through the broken fences trespassers have come in to pilfer, even to claim squatters' rights.

Augustus, three hundred years earlier, had been faced by an analogous problem. The state had been harassed for a century by internal strife, and rival dynasts had claimed their share in its spoils. Augustus, after defeating every competitor, had emerged as sole master of the state, which, sick and tired of war and the politics which led to war, was willing enough to leave the direction of affairs in the hands of this cold, capable man. Aided by a minister of outstanding ability and loyalty, Agrippa, Augustus did succeed in founding a polity which was not only viable but capable of prosperous expansion. But expansion in one direction only, the extension of the city and its amenities. What we know as the Roman empire was in essence an association of cities. Roman civilization was an urban civilization. The city remained the unit of political stature. The citizens were permitted and indeed encouraged to manage their own affairs, with the provincial governors as general supervisors. A man thought of himself as an Alexandrian, a Lyonnais or an Athenian, not as an Egyptian, a Gaul or a Greek. This concept was to persist until the last days of the empire; Ausonius, for instance, writing in the latter part of the fourth century, frequently equates Rutupiae (Richborough in Kent) with Britain, because it was at that period one of the most important towns in the island.[1]

This mode of thought was a legacy from the Greek idea of the city as state, the *polis*, the only political unit a Greek could comprehend. When the Romans supplanted the Hellenes as rulers of the Greek world they found themselves masters of a galaxy of cities, which spread from Salonika and Byzantium in the north, down through Pergamum and Ephesus to Antioch, on through

[1] *Parentalia*, VII, 2; XVIII, 8; *Aquileia*, 9.

the Decapolis (the federated Greek colonies in Semitic Phoenicia) to Alexandria. West of Alexandria there was the Greek pentapolis of Libya; farther west still, the Greek cities of Sicily and of southern Italy. There were Greek cities in Gaul, and even in Spain. This last penetration was the work of one small city. "This was Phocaea, on the coast of Asia Minor north of Smyrna, the ultimate ancestor not only of Marseilles, the greatest and most famous of all the Phocaean colonies, but also of Nice, Antibes, Alicante, Malaga and the settlements on the Balearic islands."[1]

This great ring of Hellenic urban settlement was the foundation of the Roman empire and was to remain its heart, so much so that when the west had been transformed and submerged, the Roman–Greek east survived. But even this summary of the Greek legacy does not complete the urban picture. To the Greek foundations must be added those of the Phoenicians, the great cities of the north African littoral. Carthage was deemed to have been annihilated in the year 146 B.C., but the city was to know another great flowering in the days of the Antonines; and the whole region was caressed and stimulated when the Severan dynasty became lords of the ascendant, because its founder, Septimius Severus, was an African, born at Lepcis Magna, in what is now Libya, and married to a Semite from Homs in Syria. This magnificent city of Lepcis is a lesson in three dimensions of how the Punic spirit lived on, and the neo-Punic language with it, and how both mingled with the Greek and Roman traditions. The language lasted, both in the old Phoenicia and in the new, right into the fifth century. So did Carthage. Ausonius, in his poem called *The Order of Famous Cities*, of which one, Aquileia, has already been quoted[2] opens the work with the following lines:

> *First among cities, the home of gods, is golden Rome.*
> *Carthage yields precedence to Constantinople,*
> *But will not yield a full step down, because she disdains*
> *To be counted as third, but dares not hope for the second*
> *Which both have held.*

Ausonius, who was born in Bordeaux and spent the last days of his life there, may be regarded as a fair arbiter between the claims of east and west as they were in his day. We are not surprised that Antioch and Alexandria come fourth and fifth,

---

[1] *The Greeks in the West*, A. G. Woodhead, p. 66.
[2] pp. 24, n. 1.

nor that Trèves and Milan, then both imperial residences, should be placed sixth and seventh. Aquileia is given ninth place only because, as Ausonius says, it had recently been the scene of a victory of Theodosius over the usurper Maximus; otherwise "this is not your place". Tenth is Arles, "the little Rome of Gaul". Then come four Spanish cities, Seville, Cordova, Tarragona and Braga. Only at fifteenth place do we find Athens, so far had she fallen from her great estate. Next, Catania and Syracuse represent Sicily. Toulouse "my nursing-mother", Narbonne, capital of Provence, and last, but by no means least in length of praise, his own beloved Bordeaux, end the song.

This catalogue is of the first interest, as shewing what the Roman world meant to a cultivated Bordelais who had been the tutor of a future emperor,[1] provincial governor and consul. These twenty cities were for Ausonius the civilized world.

Had he been an easterner, the list might have been different: it might have included some of the great towns of what is now Asia Minor, but in one respect we may be confident that it would have been the same – that is, in its omission of any cities in northern Europe or Britain. For the fact is that there were very few, and those few very far apart. Archaeology, so eloquent in the east and south, is silent in the north. "It is hard to find a Roman column in north-western Europe, and it is likely the medieval builders found few."[2]

Clearly, therefore, it is by the state of the cities, by their frequency and their prosperity that we can most fairly judge the condition of the empire at any given time. The predominance of "undeveloped" land in the north gives us an important clue to its relative un-Romanness, and prepares us for the fact, as it was to be proved by conflict, that this portion of the empire would have less ability, and indeed less will, to remain Roman than the rest of the empire.

When we examine this rest we notice that its history shews a really astonishing uniformity of pattern, so much so that it is not unfair to deduce a general outline of the history of the whole empire therefrom. Starting with the Augustan age, we find[3] a general consolidation of existing cities. The imperial

---

[1] Gratian, see pp. 49–50 below.

[2] Jones, p. 1065, with the note: "I cannot claim to have made an exhaustive search, but I have spotted only four re-used antique columns in northern France (in the apse of Senlis cathedral) and none in this country."

[3] To avoid a rash of footnotes, it may be explained that the following observations are based not only on a study of literary sources but on personal acquaintance with a number of classical sites, including: *Spain,*

government or its agents present such amenities as aqueducts, while grateful citizens erect temples to Augustus or to the genius of Rome. A new era of peace and prosperity starts for the Graeco-Roman world.

Under the Julio-Claudians and the Flavians, that is, the successors of Augustus down to Nero, and Vespasian and his two sons this process continues, specially as regards public works, to which the emperor Claudius in particular gave a great stimulus.

Trajan, who came from Italica, near Seville, in Spain, and his nephew and successor Hadrian, were the founders of the so-called "Antonine Age", which lasted until the death of Marcus Aurelius in the year 180. This was the golden age of Rome, and during it a quite astonishing amount of building and embellishing took place all over the empire. Much of this was the work of private citizens, or of municipalities, who wished to honour their emperor. Triumphal arches now become common in the provinces, as they had long been in the capital. Theatres, amphitheatres, temples, baths, ornamental fountains, all the amenities of Roman life now appear in dazzling profusion. Old cities are brought up to date, new ones are founded.[1] It is clear from the architectural remains no less than from the inscriptions that the cities of the empire were now well-to-do and competent to carry on the work of government. The city was the administrative centre of the *civitas*, or Urban and Rural District. A man was described not by his place of residence, but by his city of origin – so important was the urban conception of life. That is why, for instance, Joseph had to resort to Bethlehem, his *origo*, for the census, as we learn from St Luke.[2] St Paul was similarly known as "of Tarsus".[3] The cities were at this period well governed.

Seville, Italica, Tarragona, Segovia; *Africa*, Volubilis, Sabratha, Tripoli, Lepcis, Tolmeita, Teuchira, Benghazi, Cyrene, Tunis–Carthage, Sousse, Thuburbo maius, Hippo Regius, Alexandria; *Levant*, Caesarea, Jerusalem, Jericho, Amman, Jerash, Petra, Tyre, Beirut, Byblos, Baalbek, Palmyra, Damascus, Antioch; *Asia Minor*, Attalia, Perga, Side, Aspendos, Priene, Ephesus, Pergamum, Mersin, Halicarnassus, Neapolis, Troy, Istanbul; *Cyprus*, Salamis–Constantia, Curium; *Greece*, Athens, Delphi, Olympia, Eleusis, Pella, Salonika, Delos; *Sicily and Italy*, Syracuse, Catania, Taormina, Piazza Armerina, Paestum, Rome, Ostia, Milan, Ravenna.

[1] Hadrian entirely rebuilt Jerusalem, which had been destroyed by Titus in A.D. 70, as a Roman colony, Aelia Capitolina. The existing city preserves Hadrian's plan.

[2] II, 3–5.

[3] e.g. *Acts* IX, 11; XXI, 39.

Any idea of popular representation had long since faded, in the provinces as in the capital. Only in the theatre could the people, both in Rome and in provincial cities, express their feelings, and even that might be risky, as we learn again from St Luke in his description of the disturbances which marred St Paul's visit to Ephesus: the town clerk was terrified lest there might be an official enquiry into the affair.[1] Even the liberal-minded Trajan forbade the formation of a Firemen's Guild in Nicomedia of Bithynia. His friend Pliny, the governor, had written to say that there had been a fire in that city, and that no organization existed to combat such a disaster. Might he enrol a guild of not more than 150 members, whose strict attention to business he would guarantee, so small a number being easily controlled? Trajan said No: whatever title they might be given, they would become political before long.[2]

The direction of the city's affairs was in the hands of a council, a co-optive body whose members, called decurions, were elected for life. The average council numbered 500. The offices were modelled on those of Rome: two *duoviri*, who corresponded to the consuls, two *aediles*, responsible for municipal public services, water, drainage, markets and so on, two quaestors who were the city treasurers. These officers were elected annually. There would also be a number of priests of various cults and augurs.

What did these cities look like? Of this we can form a very good idea from the remains of so many of them that still survive. The general plan is surprisingly uniform: its application amazingly varied. In the second half of the fifth century B.C. there appeared in Miletus, in Asia Minor, a genius called Hippodamus, who is generally regarded as the father of town-planning.[3] The town of Priene, on the opposite side of the river Maeander, is built on the Hippodamian plan, and had the good fortune to be visited by Alexander the Great, who so much admired its design that he adopted it for his new foundations. Pericles had also commissioned Hippodamus to lay out the Peiraeus. Thus the new "grid" pattern came into general

[1] *Acts* XIX.

[2] Pliny the Younger, *Letters*, X, 33 and 34.

[3] Notably by Aristotle; although as Sir Mortimer Wheeler has shewn, "rectangular planning" was practised in the third millennium B.C. and after a considerable gap comes to light again in the seventh-century relics of Old Smyrna. "The earliest extensive traces of Greek chessboard planning recovered by excavation are (probably) at the city of Miletus itself and (certainly) at the little town of Priene."

use. As developed by the Romans, it was based on the following simple features. First, the city was sited as near a good water-supply as possible, preferably on or above the banks of some river, because the Romans, no less than the Greeks, thought that one of the prime functions of a city was to be beautiful. Next, they laid out a main street, called the *cardo maximus*, or great hinge – an apt designation, for everything turned on it. This generally ran north and south, so that the buildings on each side of it would get their fair share of sun and shade. Along this street, which might vary considerably in width, ran colonnades, and behind the colonnades rose co-ordinated buildings, temples, basilicas, fountains, shops, gymnasia. The main street was intersected at intervals with cross-streets, called *decumani*. These ran back to serve other quarters, where the dwelling-houses were grouped, and also gave access to theatres, stadia and baths. Even to-day, to walk along the main street of a town such as Ostia, Jerash, Volubilis or Priene itself, is to feel a pang of nostalgia, of regret that we no longer care to live amid such ordered amenity.

The golden age of the provincial city was prolonged in some instances, notably in Africa, by the advent of the Severan dynasty, who were themselves of African origin, and in Syria from which Septimius Severus' empress had sprung. The huge temple at Baalbek bears a dedicatory inscription to Caracalla, Septimius' son. But that temple was never finished. As the age of "iron and rust" wore on, as the third century drifted into chaos, the cities suffered. The mere physical ravages of the civil wars were appalling. Byzantium was destroyed, so was Lyons, so were many other towns. Hardly one city, specially in Gaul and the east, the empire's most prosperous regions, escaped the consequences of the growing disasters. One of the most damaging results of prolonged warfare, as our own generation knows to its cost, is inflation. The Roman currency became progressively more feeble, and the only remedy the government could think of was to debase it. This vortex began to form in the days of Caracalla, and became wider, deeper and more ravenous as the century wore on.

In times of financial instability it is always the city-dwellers who suffer first and most, because, unlike the peasant, who can live on and by his farm, the townsman has to buy his food and clothing, and to buy them in exchange for current coin. The predicament of the townsmen might not have alarmed the central government: what did alarm it was that the towns

D

became less and less able to collect and to remit their assessed taxes.

To meet this situation the government started the system of collecting taxes in kind, a system which not only led to every sort of unjust exaction, fraud and corruption but also involved the taxpayers in a new form of slavery. If an estate or a district was to produce annually the amount of goods and foodstuffs at which it was assessed it was essential that its population should remain stable. And so it was ordained that a man must follow his father's calling, be he farmer or artisan, and that he must not move from the district in which he was enrolled. Diocletian extended this rule to the army as well as to the civil population: henceforth those who had formerly been citizens were mere "units", slaves of the state.

This lamentable travesty of the commonwealth could by its nature be maintained only by an army of bureaucrats, and the bureaucrats could be maintained only by an army of slaves. The cities declined more and more, as commerce dwindled. In their place arose great rural estates, ruled in feudal style by rich landlords, who could make their own terms with the government and its predatory minions. Of such estates we have considerable knowledge from the archaeological evidence which they have left to us. There is, for instance, the vast palace at Piazza Armarina in Sicily. It is situated in open country, between Enna and Syracuse, and when it first came to light after the second world war it puzzled scholars by its remoteness, coupled with its lavish lay-out and decoration. It contains several courtyards, its own baths, colonnades, porticoes, and a remarkable series of floor mosaics, some adorned with the standard mythological subjects, others shewing hunting-scenes, and one which depicts the capture, embarkation and transport of wild animals, destined for the amphitheatre or for zoos. To account for all this magnificence a theory was put forward that it must really have been an imperial villa, a sort of second Tibur,[1] belonging to Constantine's rival Maxentius. For this there is no evidence whatsoever; nor is the hypothesis necessary. Its owner was simply one of the new class of rural tycoons whose estates were replacing the cities.[2]

There is ample evidence of the same economy in the mosaics

[1] Hadrian's famous villa, three-quarters the size of Rome itself.

[2] See Professor J. M. C. Toynbee, in *Journal of Roman Studies*, Vol. LIV (1964), Parts I and II, p. 12.

of Africa, of which magnificent collections have been assembled in the museums of Tripoli and Tunis, the latter being the finest of its kind in existence. These are of particular value, because they shew us not only what the resources and activities of the "ranches" were but also what the houses looked like. They were palatial. Like Piazza Armarina, these villas possessed their own baths, and pillared porticoes in profusion. There is literary evidence for the same sort of life in Gaul, which will be considered later on.[1] Here it will be enough to quote one line from a poet who has left us a record of a coastal cruise from Rome to a port near Genoa[2] in the year 416, that is, six years *after* the sack of Rome by Alaric. Looking back at the coast from the ship, he tells us that he passes by what are now Palo and Santa Severa – "to-day large country estates, in earlier days small towns".

There, in one line, we have the verdict: the larger towns might, and did, survive, even if on a diminished scale. The smaller ones, the very cells of the empire's life, were dead, killed by inflation, corruption and exaction. If this is not decline it is hard to say what is.[3]

So much for the material side of the internal situation: the spiritual will be considered later. But first, having dealt with the first of the two questions posed at the end of the last chapter, namely why was the bureaucracy necessary and was it good or evil, let us now turn to the second: why was the army doubled?

[1] See Chapter IX.

[2] Rutilius Namatianus: the last classical Latin poet. Of great interest: see Chapter VII below. Line 224 is here cited.

[3] For detailed and documented reviews of the process of urban decline, see Rostovtzeff, *Social and Economic History of the Roman Empire*, 1957 edn, Ch. IX; also *Cambridge Ancient History*, Vol. XII, Ch. VII. The decline affected even remote Britain: *ibid.*, pp. 283 *seq.*

CHAPTER IV

FAITHFUL UNTO DEATH?

Of all the manifestations of the Roman genius, none has caught the popular fancy more than the Roman army. Those brave, loyal, sinewy men, poised tautly along the misty frontiers of a golden empire, they were the very emblems of warm civilization confronting the cold barbarity of the savage outsiders. This picture is in nearly every respect a caricature.

Throughout the later days of the empire, the army became less Roman and less loyal. Even in its best days, those of the great Trajan and his successor Hadrian, the army had been more devoted to the ruler than to Rome. It was to the man who paid them, and not to the country who bred them, that these troops regarded themselves as beholden. They were, in fact, all mercenaries, even those born within the Roman frontiers. This basic truth was demonstrated over and over again in the later Roman empire. The soldiers would always back as candidate for the purple the son of their late ruler, if he had one. If not – and this process caused the disastrous anarchy of the third century – they would simply exalt some successful general, who, they reckoned, was more likely to enrich them than any of his competitors. Even then, they might turn against him. In the pages of Ammianus, who was himself a civilian, but served in the army for some years, we have an astonishing and depressing picture of the vicious fickleness of the army. He is constantly giving instances of the savagery, the innate brutishness, of the soldiery,[1] and of their treachery.[2] They had always, it seems, to be cajoled, not commanded.

There were three other factors that debilitated the imperial armies. The first was that their pay and perquisites were often in arrears. When they were serving in garrisons they were billeted on the population, and were entitled to occupy up to a third of a citizen's dwelling. They often occupied a good deal more, and helped themselves to what they needed in the way of food and drink. If the householder complained to the civil authority the military took measures to guarantee that he would

[1] e.g. XIV, 10, 4; XXIV, 2, 3.
[2] e.g. XVII, 9, 3, XXIV, 3, 3; XXVI, 1, 4; XXVI, 2, 4 *et al.*

protect them. Owing to the inflation, the soldier's pay, of which the nominal sum had often been increased, was but nugatory: what he depended on was loot, and periodical gifts of gold and silver from his commander; in plain language, on bribes.

The second disability of the army was that, even with conscription, it was hard to keep it up to strength. This had been the case even in the golden days of the Antonines, and later shrinkage in the population had aggravated it. During periods of oppressive maladministration, such as the later Romans experienced, people tend to breed less and less. This phenomenon was clearly noticeable both in the Ottoman empire and in its predecessor. The selling of children had become so usual in the days of Diocletian that it was officially permitted. There was even a fair held in southern Italy at which peasants regularly offered their children for sale.[1]

And yet, as native man-power declined, the demands upon it increased. As explained in the last chapter, the peasantry had become to all intents and purposes slaves, whose sole remedy, as of all slaves, was to threaten to run away. There was a technical term, even, for these "flights", or *anachoreseis* as they were called. Where, then, were the fighting men to come from? In the Roman army, as in the French and British of later days, there had for centuries been bodies of auxiliary troops drawn from "allied", that is, dependent, nations on the frontiers of the empire. They provided bowmen, slingers and other specialized arms of the service. But the legions had always been Roman, and the legions were accounted the backbone of the army. Under the Diocletianic reorganization, this distinction had been blurred: the dividing line was now that between the frontier troops and the garrison troops, who were really little more than coercive gendarmerie, when so employed. Most odious of all were the secret police, called, with that childish naïveté which distinguishes such organizations, by the simple name of *agentes in rebus*, business agents.[2] Given the facts that the demands on the frontier troops had greatly increased, that it was therefore essential to increase their numbers and that at the same time a whole swarm of military was now employed in the provinces as well, it is obvious that the army must be expanded. It is equally clear, from the facts related above, that the necessary men could come only from the

---

[1] Jones, p. 1043.
[2] cf. the modern French use of the word *agent*.

"allies", that is from races other than the Romans. The army thus became ever more cosmopolitan and less likely to be animated by any genuine patriotism.

We happen to possess the archives of an Egyptian soldier called Abinnaeus,[1] who was officer commanding the garrison of Dionysias, in the Fayyûm in Egypt in the middle of the fourth century. His troops consisted of a wing of cavalry. They were stationed in a large fortress which has been identified and excavated. It is almost a hundred metres square, with walls seven metres high, and nearly four metres thick. In itself, this building is of interest as being an example of the standard model of fort which was planted by Diocletian along the borders of the whole empire. But, we at once ask ourselves, what was such a fortress doing in the peaceful Fayyûm, in the heart of peaceful and fertile Egypt? The archives soon tell us. Many of the documents preserved – there are eighty-two of them – deal with the day-to-day chores of public security, battery, theft, trespass, smuggling. One, asking headquarters to send some nets to trap the gazelles which are nibbling the crops, is a precious miniature of the eternal Egypt. But, in the words of the editors, "The *alae*, like the cohortes, were called on for service against brigands and smugglers, and, even more, to control the inhabitants of the country."[2] Of these police duties, "our papyri reveal three principal ones, recruiting, the annona (corn supply) and the administration of justice". It was the army who had to make sure that each group of little farms, known as a *capitulum*, furnished the prescribed number of recruits, or their equivalent in cash: it was a civil obligation, but how could so odious an exaction be enforced by any government, be it Roman or Ottoman, except by armed insistence? In just the same way, it must be the army which would ensure that the peasants' threshing-floors were denuded to maintain the civil and military administrations, and the requisite quota of grain forwarded to Constantinople. The administration of justice is the civil function *par excellence*; but here again to such a pass had things come that "in matters of justice as in fiscal matters, in the immediate zone of a military station, military authority tended, for convenience and contrary to legal dispositions, to take the place of civil authority".

[1] Beautifully published by the Clarendon Press in 1962 as *The Abinnaeus Archive*, Papers of a Roman Officer in the Reign of Constantius II, collected and edited by H. I. Bell, V. Martin, E. G. Turner, D. Van Berchem.
[2] p. 16.

The third drawback from which the army suffered – internally, that is, not strategically – was its old-fashioned outlook and equipment. The military mind tends in all ages to be conservative. That is why when on rare occasions some new device is brought into action it has such spectacular results. The Macedonian phalanx and the Roman legion, which overthrew it, are two examples. Having won the battle of Cynoscephalae in 197 B.C., thereby proving that the legion was superior to the phalanx, the Romans evolved no new military techniques,[1] until in the third century they were compelled to by the Persians. This is an important point to remember when discussing, as we shall shortly be, the age-long strife between Rome and Persia. The Persians were the only civilization, after the eclipse and absorption of Hellas, that Rome came in contact with. In the arts and in organization it was at least Rome's equal. In military technique it was Rome's superior. The Persians, brought up on the plains of what is now Iraq as their battleground, a region so flat that an Arab astronomer would calculate the length of a degree of the earth's circumference on it, evolved a method of mounted warfare which was a match for the legions. They employed two sorts of cavalry, the analogue of the modern tank and aeroplane respectively. The heavy cavalry were clad from head to foot in metal and were called *cataphracti*.[2] The light cavalry were armed with bows, and accompanied by men on dromedaries with relays of arrows. They could approach a hostile concentration, send a shower of arrows into their ranks and then again, as they galloped off, turn round and shoot another volley – the famous

---

[1] Marius had widened the basis of recruitment, and had introduced improved weapons and disposition – but that had been in 100 B.C.

[2] Cataphracts were not new. Tacitus tells us (*Hist.*, I, lxxix) that the nobles and princes of the Sarmatians were clad in plated mail, and their horses as well. In fact, many of Rome's enemies in Europe and Asia employed cataphracts. The name is Greek, and we know that Alexander's successors encountered and employed them. But it was the Persians who originated and perfected the cataphract. In A.D. 165 Fronto, writing to Lucius Verus, who was campaigning in the east, says they were like "scaled monsters of the sea". Ammianus (XXIV, 4, 15) says the metal plates of the Persian cataphracts were so skilfully compacted that they looked like "a thin layer of feathers". The Romans were certainly employing cataphracts by the time of Aurelian, i.e. c. 270 (*Aug. Hist.*, XI, 4; XXXIV, 4.). The Roman *catafractarii* were sometimes called *clibanarii*, a word which seems to be derived from a word meaning "oven" or "iron box", a vivid indication of what it must have felt like to be so clad, specially in the Levant.

"Parthian shot". This method of warfare, too, the Romans were bound to imitate and they did; but it must always be borne in mind that in wars between Rome and Persia it was the Persians who enjoyed the prestige of priority, of being the pioneers, and the moral advantage which that bestows. On the other hand, when it came to siege warfare there was little to choose between the two powers. The methods of investment, of attack and counter-thrust, of towers, ramps, rams, catapults and mines had remained unchanged over the centuries. The vivid descriptions of sieges which Ammianus gives us read exactly like those of Josephus three hundred years earlier.

Having now briefly indicated the disadvantages with which the army was laden, namely, lack of loyalty, lack of money, lack of man-power and lack of technical enterprise, it will be appropriate to describe what the tasks were which it had to face – apart from the gendarmerie duties mentioned above.

The main preoccupations of the Roman armies in the fourth century were what they had been in the first, that is, the maintenance of the frontiers in the north and in the east. The north meant the tribes beyond the Rhine and the Danube, the east meant Persia; but by the time which we are treating the difficulties on both fronts had enormously increased. To take the east first: in the year 53 B.C. a Roman army had been defeated by the Parthians,[1] seven legions cut to pieces, their standards lost and 10,000 prisoners led away to captivity. The standards and the prisoners, what was left of them, were recovered by Augustus through diplomacy. The poets sang of the glorious transaction; but the sting of this defeat remained. Fortunately for Rome the Parthian power declined, and it was not until the days of Marcus Aurelius that any Persian was seen west of the River Euphrates except as a suppliant or a hostage.[2] Yet the threat remained, and so the legions had to remain in the east to meet it. It is a strange and baffling fact that the Romans never did succeed in coming to a real understanding with their eastern neighbours. From the beginning they had underrated them: it was Pompey's double-dealing with them that had antagonized their king, as the victorious Persian

---

[1] The Arsacids, who established their kingdom on the débris of the domains of the Seleucids, Alexander's Graeco-Persian successors, in the third century B.C.

[2] Trajan invaded Mesopotamia and carried Roman arms as far as the Persian gulf – quite uselessly. Hadrian abandoned the new territories. See p. 18 above.

general reminded the defeated Crassus. National pride was involved. The Romans were used to pushing their neighbours around, and did not see why the Parthians should be any exception. The Persians, on the other hand, were not going to be treated like "natives". Both sides had everything to gain by peaceful co-existence, if only because so much of the immensely valuable Indian and Chinese trade passed through Persia into Roman-controlled entrepôts. But the quarrel went on, usually over the question who was to rule Armenia, to which both powers claimed the right of nominating a sovereign.

In the year 199 Septimius Severus inflicted further defeats on the Parthians, but, as things turned out, it was Rome which suffered, because the enfeeblement of the Parthians led to the rise of a far more powerful dynasty, the Sassanians. Their founder, Ardashir, was bent on reviving the glories of the Achaemenids, and of ruling once again not only Mesopotamia but Syria, Egypt and Asia Minor as well. In 234 the Romans quelled Ardashir, as they did his successor Shapur in 241; but in 260 the emperor Valerian was captured with all his army, and died as a Persian slave, a humiliation of which the rock-cut memorials still survive.

The war was renewed by Diocletian in 297; and there were again prolonged but not continuous hostilities from the days of Constantius in 337 until the defeat and death of Julian in 363. The key city of Nisibis was besieged in 338, 346 and 350. In 360 Amida was captured. The disgraceful capitulation made by Jovian, Julian's transient successor – he reigned for eight months only – surrendered five provinces beyond the Tigris, together with Nisibis and Sinjar, which had been Roman since the days of Septimius Severus. There was more fighting in 368. Thereafter, except for two brief wars under Theodosius II, in 421 and 440, the frontier was quiescent for more than a hundred years; but the basic threat remained. The sixth century saw a disastrous renewal of the strife. From 502 to 506, 527 to 532, the two empires were at war. In 540 Antioch was sacked, largely because the eastern front had been drained to provide troops for Belisarius' conquest of Africa. This war did not end until 561, only to be renewed for another twenty years in 571. The apocalyptic climax came in 613, when the Persians overran the whole of the Levant and Egypt, too, thus fulfilling a part at least of Ardashir's dream, and occupying lands which their ancestors had ruled more than a millennium before. The damage they did was enormous, and Palestine never really recovered from it. Heraclius won the last round of the secular struggle in 629, just before both the antagonists went down before the invading Muslims in the next decade.

So ended one of the most futile, lamentable and disastrous oppositions in all recorded history. Two great civilizations, which could have done so much in harmony, were consumed by what the Roman historian Sallust calls the *libido dominandi*,[1] the lust for domination. Of the many factors that contributed to the decline of Rome this eastern ulcer was one of the most mortal.

When we turn to the northern frontier we are confronted by a scene no less bleak, but far more complex. Here it is not a question of the opposition of two great rivals, two clearly defined world powers for ever at odds; it is rather a story of gradual shifts of pressure, according to the direction and force of the wind, of slow erosion here and there, until finally the dykes are breached irreparably.

Our study of this process is hampered by two facts. The first is that we know so little about the tribes who were the invaders; the second is that not all of those who entered the Roman pale were invaders: many of them were refugees. These two factors are inter-related. Generally speaking, all tribal movements towards the Mediterranean have come from the north, that is, from cold to warm. It was thus that the Greeks arrived in Greece, in two waves, one in the second millennium B.C. (the Achaeans), the second in the eleventh century B.C. (the Dorians). The idea that the Greeks were the result of a "tribal invasion" may seem rather shocking, but that is in fact what they were, or, rather, of two tribal invasions. The process was to be continuous, until Rome felt herself strong enough to arrest it. This she did in the year 390 B.C., but only just: the Gauls had ravaged Italy and Rome itself, where the Capitol alone held out, to turn the scales. In 108 B.C. the Teutons and the Cimbri invaded Provence: it took the great Marius, the man who remodelled the Roman army, to repel them. Just what induced these tribes and their successors to move south exactly when they did, we cannot tell: we see the actors in the limelight of history only when they have stepped on to the stage; how they approached it we do not know. In some cases, beyond doubt, they had been forced into action by other tribes, farther to the north, or even to the east, Slavs or Chinese. Ammianus

---

[1] Sallust, *Catiline*, II, 2. Augustine quotes the phrase more than once in his *City of God*. For him it was the besetting sin of imperial Rome.

tells us[1] that the Chinese protected their territory with lofty walls, a reference no doubt to the Great Wall. This obstacle excluded the Scythians, who accordingly turned west, and so started the pressure series that, at the other end of the long line, was to harass the Romans. That the Great Wall of China should have affected the fortunes of Rome may seem fantastic, but even in those days nations and events were more interrelated than is often allowed.

It was this pressure which brought into play the second of the two factors mentioned above. Many of the tribesmen sought within the Roman pale not loot, but livelihood, not plunder, but peace, now denied them in their own lands by the "squeeze" of the new arrivals. The northerners were, as their descendants still are, among the best soldiers in the world; and it was natural that a Rome which was already feeling the man-power shortage should welcome them into her armies.

The next scene in the drama illustrates all the points made above. In the year 9 B.C. Augustus sent as governor of "Germany", that is, a newly formed province on the Rhine, a man called Quintilius Varus. Varus started treating the high-spirited Germans as "natives". Not only did he try to "Romanize" them with tactless speed but he also, so Dio Cassius tells us,[2] began "issuing orders to them as if they were slaves of the Romans". The result was that as Varus was returning with three legions from an expedition to the Weser, he was set on by a German chieftain called Armin, in the Teutobergre marshes, and utterly defeated, his army being cut to pieces.

This battle was reckoned by Creasy, in his famous book, as one of the fifteen decisive battles of history, because it put an end to any possible expansion of Roman arms and empire in lands beyond the Rhine. Many people have lamented that result ever since, particularly Frenchmen, who have had more cause than most to regret that Germans never absorbed Roman civilization. As late as 1950, Daniel-Rops could write: "the 'wisdom' of Tiberius and Hadrian which their contemporaries eulogized so, stupidly abandoned the project of occupying Germany, Central Europe, Caledonia and Ireland, although such a project was still perfectly possible".[3]

How perfectly impossible it was, let Dio Cassius explain. Augustus was appalled at the disaster (Dio tells us), and not

---

[1] XXIII, 6, 64.
[2] LVI, 18.
[3] *The Church in the Dark Ages*, English translation, p. 55.

only appalled but terrified. He expected the victorious Germans to press on into Italy, and to Rome itself, because Augustus knew well that once the frontier line was breached, there was nothing to stop them – a fact of Roman military life that was to be demonstrated over and over again. Nor could new troops be raised "because there were no citizens of military age worth mentioning". Already, in the very springtime of the empire, the fatal shortage manifested itself. So did something else. Dio goes on to say that Augustus "feared a rebellion of the Gauls and Germans in the praetorian guard" and took steps to see that they were posted to distant stations.[1] Augustus never got over this disaster. To the end of his days he kept the anniversary as a day of mourning, and could be heard to murmur, as he wandered about alone at night: "Quintilius Varus, give me back my legions."[2]

The fatal success of one single penetration, the impossibility of raising new Roman forces, and the dependence on foreign ones – all these three factors are to be found in this one episode, which has been analysed by a contemporary scholar as follows:[3] "Augustus set out to conquer Germany, and failed. He lost an army and advised his successors to abandon the idea of conquest. That decision was the watershed in the development of classical antiquity; hitherto it had been a history of continuous expansion, from the spreading colonies of Aegean Greece and the conquests of Alexander to the recent annexations of Julius Caesar. From A.D. 9 it ceased to expand territorially, apart from frontier rectifications, and spent its energies on internal expansion."

As noted above, the tribal pressure was sporadic, depending as often as not on events in the dim periphery of the world. But, as in the east, the peril persisted, and so the frontier must be manned. The great column of Trajan in Rome to this day expounds the victories he won fighting the Dacians in A.D. 101–3 and 107–8: that of Marcus Aurelius near by, his triumphs over the Germans in 171–3 and the Sarmatians during the next two years. It was not in a secluded study, but in a cold campaigner's tent that the philosopher-emperor wrote the greater part of his famous *Meditations*, to such a pass already had the empire come.

So far, though, frequent as the incursions had been, the

---

[1] Dio Cassius, LVI, 23.
[2] Suetonius, *Deified Augustus*, XXIII.
[3] John Morris, *Past and Present*, No 29, p. 192.

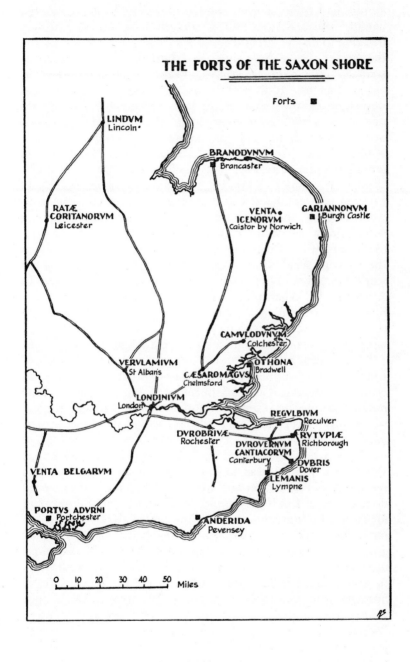

THE FORTS OF THE SAXON SHORE

Forts ■

LINDVM
Lincoln

BRANODVNVM
Brancaster

RATÆ
CORITANORVM
Leicester

VENTA
ICENORVM
Caistor by Norwich

GARIANNONVM
Burgh Castle

CAMVLODVNVM
Colchester

VERVLAMIVM
St Albans

CÆSAROMAGVS
Chelmsford

OTHONA
Bradwell

LONDINIVM
London

REGVLBIVM
Reculver

DVROBRIVÆ
Rochester

RVTVPIÆ
Richborough

DVROVERNVM
CANTIACORVM
Canterbury

DVBRIS
Dover

VENTA BELGARVM

LEMANIS
Lympne

PORTVS ADVRNI
Portchester

ANDERIDA
Pevensey

0   10   20   30   40   50   Miles

empire had been vigorous enough to repulse them; but in the age of "iron and rust" which followed it became increasingly less able to do so. To make matters worse for the Romans, the barbarians, for so long dissipated into tribes, now began to coalesce into military groups; Franks, Alamans, Vandals, Goths, Saxons. It was these last who were to menace and devastate our own country, to such an extent that a special officer was appointed to repel them. He was called the Count of the Saxon shore, and commanded the fortresses of which Rutupiae (Richborough) and Caistor, near Norwich, are among the best preserved. The whole chain stretched from the Wash to Portsmouth Harbour. In 258 the Alamans and Franks ravaged not only Gaul but northern Italy and even Spain as well. Nor was the east immune. In the year 260 the Roman command of the Mediterranean, unchallenged for three hundred years, was infringed by the Goths, who boldly sailed down the coast of Asia Minor and attacked Ephesus, wrecking the world-famous temple of Diana. Seven years later they were in Athens itself. When they were about to burn one of its many libraries a tribesman "respected for his wisdom" dissuaded them, saying that the Athenians would be easier to beat if they were buried in old books than if they had swords in their hands.

So the erosion by the barbarians went on, and so, with it, went on the recruitment of barbarians to prevent it. This is not quite so paradoxical as it might sound to modern ears, because it must always be borne in mind that although the Roman world was subject to many afflictions, one scourge which it escaped was nationalism. The tribesmen from first to last had no desire whatsoever to set up their own fragmentary states. What they wanted was to enter the Roman state, the sole repository of civilization and wealth. If necessary, they would do it by force; but if they could do it peacefully, and get paid for it into the bargain, so much the better. Thus we find an increasing military intake from foreign nations and whole groups of foreigners settled within the Roman frontiers at their own request. We read, for instance, that the emperor Gratian, in 378, enlisted in his own forces a group of young German hostages as soon as they had been handed over, and that eight years earlier a group of German prisoners were sent to Italy, "where they received fertile cantons, and now live as our subjects on the banks of the Po".[1] Each of these examples is but one of many. As the fourth century wears on, we find the army

[1] Ammianus, XXXI, 10, 17; and XXVIII, 5, 15.

more and more not only composed of foreign recruits but commanded by them. Many of these generals had adopted Roman names, such as Victor, Magnentius or Sylvanus, but others, such as Merobaud, Dagalaif, Bauto and Ricimer, clearly proclaim their origin. At the court of Constantius the Franks were numerous and influential,[1] while twenty years later we are told that it was a rare event that all the generals in one region should be Romans.[2] Nor are we surprised to learn that during the siege of Adrianople by the Goths in 378, three hundred Roman infantry suddenly went over to the other side, by whom (no doubt as the result of some old tribal vendetta) they were at once killed.[3] In that same year Valens himself was killed in battle with the Goths.

One emperor had met his death fighting in the east, another in the west. The barbarians were settled within the empire, they were powerful at court, they were dominant in the army. Was it to be expected that, when barbarian arms challenged the inviolability of Rome itself, the Eternal City would withstand these mortal enemies?

[1] Ammianus, XV, 5, 11.
[2] *Ibid.*, XXXI, 16, 8.
[3] *Ibid.*, XXXI, 15, 4.

CHAPTER V

FROM DIOCLETIAN TO ALARIC

Before we come to deal with the great catastrophe itself, it may be helpful to have an outline of the years that led up to it, a purely secular framework, as it were, on which to hang the many-coloured web of Rome's history in the fourth century of our era.

When in the year 305 Diocletian retired to his fortress-palace at Split (see p. 14) he had conferred on the Roman dominions one great boon, namely internal tranquillity. Despite all the defects to which attention has been drawn in the preceding chapters, despite, too, the spiritual malady which is discussed in Chapter VI, the citizens enjoyed peace and security, a respite from the miseries of civil war. But not even that negative solace was to be theirs for long. Vainly would they implore their gods "lest intermitted vengeance arm again His red right hand to plague us". For as soon as Diocletian's authority was withdrawn, the Tetrarchy dissolved. The quadrumvirate consisted (see p. 16) of two Augusti, Diocletian and Maximian, and two Caesars, Constantius in the west and Galerius in the east. When on 1st May, 305, the two Augusti abdicated the two Caesars automatically became Augusti. The question was, who would be the new Caesars? It was generally expected that Constantine, son of Constantius by his first wife Helena, would be one. He had been betrothed to Fausta, Maximian's daughter, ever since the year 293. Nevertheless, and despite the fact that coins had recently been minted at Alexandria inscribed *Constantinus Caesar*,[1] Constantine was passed over. So was Maxentius, Maximian's son. The Caesars were to be two creatures of Galerius, named Severus and Daia.

Constantine at once realized what had happened: Galerius aimed at becoming sole emperor, after eliminating Constantius and his son, whom Galerius detained at Nicomedia as a hostage. When Constantius asked his brother Augustus to send him Constantine to help him in Gaul and Britain (where as usual the natives were giving trouble) the request could hardly be refused, specially as Constantine was already a tried soldier.

[1] *Cambridge Medieval History*, Vol. I, p. 3.

Nevertheless, as the young man was quick to appreciate, Galerius could easily tip off Severus, who controlled Gaul, to obstruct or even kill Constantine on the way. He was taking no chances: he suddenly left the palace, more a fugitive than a prince, rode hell for leather across Europe, killing the post-horses behind him to avoid pursuit, and succeeded in joining his father at Boulogne. Together they crossed into Britain, where they defeated Carausius, the upstart pretender, and after humbling the Picts returned to York. Here, on 25th July of the year 306, Constantius died. His troops at once acclaimed Constantine, not as Caesar, but as Augustus. "The army of Britain (always the most mutinous in the Empire) had no mind to wait for a new Caesar from the East. Its chief mover was Crocus the Alamannic king: and this would seem to be the first case of a barbarian king as a Roman general, and also the first case of barbarian action in the election of an emperor."[1]

Galerius, when he was shewn the portrait of Constantine crowned with laurel, was furious. He at once dubbed Severus Augustus, thus relegating Constantine to the inferior rank of Caesar. Whereupon Maxentius, not to be outdone by Constantine, had himself proclaimed Augustus by the Praetorians and persuaded his father Maximian to come out of retirement to help him. There were thus now no less than *four Augusti* in the west – Constantine, Maxentius, Severus and Maximian – and *two more* – Galerius and Daia – in the east.

Clearly this chaos could not last. The first to go was Severus, killed by Maximian. Galerius replaced him by his old comrade Licinius. Maximian next fell out with his son, and took refuge with Constantine, whom he acknowledged as Augustus, and to whom he gave his daughter Flavia in marriage. A little later, the contriving dotard, after failing to dethrone his son, sought to involve his daughter in a plot against Constantine. The plot was discovered and Maximian was constrained to commit suicide. Diocletian, growing his cabbages at Salonae, had chosen the better part.

With the death of Galerius in 311, the number of emperors was reduced to four, that is *Constantine* controlled Gaul and Britain, *Maxentius* Italy, Spain and Africa, *Licinius* Illyricum, Greece and Thrace, *Daia* the lands beyond the Bosphorus. Maxentius now decided to rely on Daia's ability to contain Licinius, while he himself eliminated Constantine, who had given his sister to Licinius in marriage.[2] Constantine at once

[1] *Ibid.*   [2] See Appendix II.

took the initiative. Leaving his headquarters at Colmar, and taking with him a small picked force, so as not to enfeeble the watch on the Rhine, he headed south. Near Turin, his Gauls defeated Maxentius' heavy cavalry. Verona was captured after a memorable siege, and the road to Rome lay open. It was during the journey thither that Constantine had the religious experience which resulted in his bidding his army to fight under the sign of the Cross, an event of which the incalculable results will be discussed below.

For Constantine all now turned on whether Maxentius would be content to remain within the walls of Rome, as he had twice done before, in which case Constantine would have been unable to besiege the City with his small army. Fortunately, Maxentius decided to march out and attack Constantine. The two armies met just north of the Milvian bridge over the Tiber. Maxentius was routed, and he and most of his troops perished in the river. Surrounded by his triumphant Gauls, Constantine entered the City. That was on 28th October, 312. Early in 313, Constantine left Rome for Milan, where the marriage of his sister Constantia to Licinius was to be solemnized. It was here that the two Augusti issued their famous edict of toleration, which for the first time permitted complete religious freedom throughout the empire. The marriage festivities were interrupted, in operatic fashion, by the news that Daia had invaded Europe and was besieging Byzantium. Licinius hastened to the east, defeated Daia near Adrianople and raised the siege. Daia committed suicide at Tarsus.

The number of the Augusti was now reduced to two; but the imperial game of beggar-my-neighbour was not yet played out. Constantine and Licinius were temperamentally poles apart. Constantine was now a convinced believer in the efficacy of the Christian God: Licinius held by the old pantheon. The two brothers-in-law quarrelled in 314. Ten years later came the final clash, precipitated by Licinius' persecution of the Christians, despite his undertaking at Milan eleven years before. Also, two years earlier, Constantine, in repelling a Gothic raid, had crossed the territory of Licinius, which led to war. After a tremendous naval battle in the straits, Byzantium was captured; Licinius, defeated in a land battle on the Asiatic shore, surrendered. At the supplication of Constantia, his life was spared; but in 325 he and his Caesar Martinianus were executed, ostensibly on a charge of plotting against the state. The young man from York was now lord of the Roman world.[1] He was to remain as such for another thirteen years: his achievement would endure for a millennium. First, there is his establishment of the Christian religion as the preferred faith of the state. To what extent Constantine understood Christianity will be discussed in its place. That it was potent as a motive force in the hearts of men and women – that he grasped beyond equivocation. He was baptized on his deathbed: "Let there be no ambiguity," he said. He devoted much of his great energy to an attempt to reconcile the various theological tendencies of his subjects.

Subjects they now were, no longer citizens. Constantine was the first to be the sole monarch of the empire, by the grace of God. It was this assumption, coupled with the affirmation of the hereditary principle, that enabled the Constantinian polity to live for a thousand years. The east had always been used to kings, and to hereditary kings. The new régime was for them but a belated return to the old.

The centre of this sovereignty was no longer republican Rome, but the new creation of Constantinople, the city built on the impregnable bastion of Byzantium, on that narrow strait which divides the west from the east. Constantine said of his creation that he had "bestowed upon it an eternal name by the commandment of God".[2]

In 325 Constantine forbade gladiatorial contests, thus providing a useful if small reservoir of man-power for the army.

In military affairs, Constantine's chief innovation was the creation of the strategic reserve, the field army under the command of two newly created officers, the master of the infantry and the master of the cavalry, who ranked with but after the praetorian prefects. He also increased the number of the auxiliary troops, recruited from federated tribesmen, as Gurkhas would be enlisted by a later empire.

Constantine also created a new nobility, the *Comites* or Counts. The word means simply companion, and the title was bestowed on those who in a military or civil capacity were employed in positions of eminence and trust.

One of Constantine's greatest achievements was the stabilization of the currency. He put into circulation a gold coin called a *solidus*; and so solid was it that it maintained its weight and purity right down to the eleventh century. One pound

---

[1] He was now, according to Berenson's reckoning, thirty-six: see *The Arch of Constantine: The Decline of Form*, p. 57.

[2] Jones, p. 83.

of gold produced seventy-two of these coins.[1] Where did the gold come from? Partly from taxation, which was now exacted in gold and silver. But chiefly, apparently, from the confiscated treasures of pagan temples. There is abundant evidence that these shrines had for centuries been the repositories of lavish accumulations of bullion, dues, *ex votos*, conscience money and ostentation. All this was now put into circulation, with a result comparable to that produced by Alexander's liberation of the hoarded treasure of the Persian kings.

When Constantine died he left behind him a great patrimony. He had established the Christian religion, he had founded a new capital which was to last for a thousand years, he had created an efficient army, and he had stabilized the currency on a gold standard.

As his successors, the army, as usual, were determined to have none but his own sons. His half-brothers, and other possible aspirants, they murdered. His sons were called Constantine, Constantius and Constans.[2] Their father, despite his great public benefactions, had shewn himself bloody and tyrannical in his family life. He had killed his wife, Fausta, and his son Crispus, besides a number of his friends. This moral blemish was to recur in his descendants. Constantine II was the first to go, overcome by Constans, who was himself eliminated by a palace revolution in 350. By the end of the next year Constantius was, like his father, the sole ruler of the empire. He was moody, vain, susceptible and suspicious.[3] He appointed a cousin, Gallus, as his Caesar, and then killed him, replacing him with his half-brother, Julian. The years 354–356 were taken up with campaigns against the Alamans, who combined with the Franks to ravage Gaul. His visit to Rome in 357 has already been described.[4]

Constantius died in 361, but more than a year before his death the army of Gaul had declared Julian Augustus. Both as a general and as an administrator he had already proved himself in Gaul, which he had cleared of the invaders and re-established financially. He is generally known to posterity by the title "apostate", because he tried to restore the old pagan

---

[1] See Note 2 on p. 97.

[2] See Appendix II.

[3] It is almost uncanny how early in the Byzantine régime occur all the qualities which were to mark the Ottoman sultans right down to the last active one, 'Abdulhamid II.

[4] pp. 5 *seq.*

pantheon and its cults. In retrospect, we may be grateful to him for having done so, because nothing could have proved more conclusively how utterly outmoded they were. The whole experiment reads like an account of a "revival" by some decrepit artist who refuses to recognize that her day is long since past. The clever folk of Antioch laughed at him, this serious young prig. He died in action against the Persians, after a reign of only eighteen months. The house of Constantine was now extinct. The election therefore lighted upon a jolly young officer called Jovian. It was he who made the humiliating terms with the Persians already referred to.[1] He died within eight months. Jovian had perforce been elected on the battlefield; but he had been peacefully elected, by agreement. So now on his death, the great officers of state, civil and military, met at Nicaea and once more agreed on their choice, that of a Pannonian soldier called Valentinian, aged forty-three. He reigned for twelve years, dying in 375. As his colleague he chose his younger brother Valens.

Valentinian was the son of a peasant, and despite his ability as a soldier remained a boor to the end of his days. Ammianus gives a very unflattering picture of him.[2] It is in his reign that the growing cult of brutality begins to show itself. The emperors were professed Christians, and yet, by a shocking paradox, their judicial processes became far more savage than those of their pagan predecessors. Absolute power had corrupted them absolutely. Torture had been allowed in Roman judicial proceedings only on the persons of slaves, and even that had been progressively mollified under the humane emperors of the second century. But now that every subject was a slave we read of men and women being condemned to be racked, furrowed with hooks, disjointed by weights, as a matter of normal legal procedure. Burning alive had by now become a common sentence.

In the year 367, when recovering from a serious illness, Valentinian had appointed his son Gratian as Caesar. Valens was killed at Adrianople fighting the united armies of the Goths in 378, whereon Gratian found himself sole emperor. As his brother Augustus he chose Theodosius, the son of a former master of the cavalry, who had distinguished himself in both Africa and Britain, but was later executed as the result of a palace intrigue. The army had also associated with him Valentinian's four-year-old son, also called Valentinian.

[1] p. 37.   [2] XXX, 8.

Theodosius has been justly called "the last of the great emperors".[1] His task was formidable. He had somehow to fill the gaps left in the army after the disaster of Adrianople. Every civilian *embusqué* of military age was enrolled. Those who amputated their thumbs to avoid service were no longer, as in the preceding reign, burnt alive, they were enlisted, but those who offered them as recruits had to give two of them in lieu of one whole man. Theodosius sharply accelerated the process whereby entire units were recruited from external tribes. Moreover, the Visigoths were actually allotted lands within the empire in Thrace and Macedonia while being still allowed to govern themselves by tribal custom. This innovation had disastrous consequences. Civil war added to the difficulties of the declining state. Gratian antagonized the armies by shewing undue favour to a newly raised foreign regiment – they were Alans – so that when the army of Britain, mutinous as usual, proclaimed as Augustus a Spanish officer called Magnus Maximus, who set about the invasion of Gaul, Gratian's soldiers simply deserted him, which led to his capture and death, on 25th August, 383.

Theodosius had perforce to recognize Maximus as his co-ruler, but after three years the civil war was renewed. Finally, in 387, Maximus capitulated and was executed. But trouble was not at an end by any means. Theodosius had proclaimed his elder son Arcadius Augustus in 383, and then sent Valentinian to Gaul, in the custody of a Frankish *magister militum* called Arbogast. Arbogast killed Valentinian, and proclaimed as Augustus a Roman professor of rhetoric. In 394 Theodosius defeated this couple at the battle of the Frigidus, an engagement notable for the fact that it eliminated the last pagan ever to aspire to the mastery of Rome. Within five months, Theodosius died at Milan, leaving the empire to his two sons, Arcadius and Honorius, Arcadius to govern the east, and Honorius the west. With the death of Theodosius and the advent of his two children, the shades of the long night gather fast.

The two Augusti were mere children, the younger, Arcadius, only ten. By the side of each, therefore, their prudent father had placed a man of experience and resolution. Arcadius' tutor was called Rufinus, a cobbler's son from the Pyrenees, who had made his way by cynical determination. Honorius was committed to a man of much finer temper, Stilicho the Vandal. The two men hated each other. Thus, just at the very

[1] Daniel-Rops, *op. cit.*, p. 65.

crisis of affairs, when east and west should have been united, they were instead ranged against each other; when they should have stood shoulder to shoulder in the face of barbarian on-slaughts, they preferred to use those very barbarians to humble each other. Arcadius died in 408, leaving his throne to his son, Theodosius II, aged seven. Honorius survived until 423, but his nephew Valentinian III was only six when he was made Augustus two years later. These prolonged minorities encouraged court intrigues, and the selfish manoeuvres of slaves and eunuchs, "while Ladies interpose, and Slaves debate". The ladies did interpose: they had far more character than the men. Pulcheria, the elder sister of Theodosius, was, like her brother, a paragon of piety, but she also had a good head for affairs, which she directed for some time. Galla Placidia, half-sister of Honorius and mother of Valentinian III, ruled the empire for ten years during her son's minority. This remarkable woman is one of a galaxy of ladies who shewed how resolute and effective women could be, in both religious and secular affairs. They are a wholly new pheno-menon: intriguing empresses there had been before, from Livia, Augustus' overbearing mate, to Julia Domna, Septimius Severus' wife, and her two kinswomen, the mothers of Elega-balus and Alexander. But with the dawn of the new age, royal ladies abandoned the boudoir for the council-chamber, and, moreover, thought nothing of undertaking long and arduous journeys in pursuit of spiritual or worldly advance-ment. In the former category the great original was Helena, mother of Constantine, who went to Jerusalem to supervise the building of churches on the sacred sites. She was followed towards the end of the century by devout women from Rome and even one from Spain, who were determined to visit the Holy Land.

On the secular side, Galla Placidia must claim pre-eminence. Her story is more like that of one of Sir Walter Scott's heroines than of an historical figure. It is worth outlining her career, because, in its variety, its ups and downs, its geographical diffuseness, it is an epitome of the distraught age in which she lived.

Galla Placidia was born about 386, the daughter of Theodo-sius I, and so half-sister to Honorius, at whose side in Ravenna we find her in 402. In 410 she seems to have advised the death of Serena, Theodosius' niece and adopted daughter and wife of Stilicho. Stilicho himself – the one man who might have saved Rome from Alaric – had been executed in 408. When Alaric sacked Rome in 410, among the booty he carried off was Galla Placidia herself. She was married to Alaric's brother-in-law, Ataulf, and went with him to Spain, where he established himself as king. When in 415 Ataulf was assassinated, Galla Placidia went back to Italy, and in the following year married an Illyrian chieftain and general called Constantius at Ravenna. In 419 she gave birth to the future Valentinian III; in 421 both she and Constantius were declared Augusti by Honorius, with whom, however, Galla Placidia quarrelled and was relegated to Byzantium. Honorius died the next year, and back went Galla Placidia to Ravenna, to act as regent for Valentinian III, and to take a prominent part in the intrigues between Aetius and Boniface which were to result in the loss of Africa to the Vandals. Galla Placidia died in 450, and was buried in St Peter's at Rome. Whether she was later transferred to the beautiful tomb which bears her name in Ravenna,[1] or whether that is the sepulchre of Constantius only is not certain.

Her daughter, Honoria, inherited her mother's flair for desegregated romance as an instrument of policy: she is recorded to have written a love-letter to Attila enclosing a ring, on the strength of which Attila was to claim a share in the rule of the empire.

It was in this autumnal world, where the storms whirled human lives about like falling leaves, that the drama of Alaric was played out. It was in or about 370 that the Huns first enter history. How terrifying and disgusting they were, both Ammianus and the poet Claudian have told us.[2] Driving westwards from the steppes, they first of all overcame the Alans, then the Ostrogoths. By 373 it was the turn of the Visigoths. Unable to withstand the Huns, they sought alliance with Rome. When that was rejected they were forced to take arms against her. That is how Valens came to lose his life at the battle of Adrianople. The victories of Theodosius, aided by two Frankish generals Bauto and Arbogast, succeeded in driving the Goths northward, and so saved the eastern provinces. In 381 the Gothic king did homage to the emperor. In the west, as already recorded, Theodosius had suppressed the British usurper, Maximus; and Arbogast recovered Gaul,

---

[1] See p. 86.

[2] See Ammianus, XXXI, 2, 1–12 seq.: Claudian Against Rufinus I, 11 323 seq.

in 388. Four years later he contrived the murder of Valentinian II, and set up a puppet called Eugenius in his place. Once again, Theodosius saved the cause of legitimacy, at the battle of the Frigidus, mentioned above. Arbogast committed suicide.

After the death of Theodosius in 395 we have already seen that power became the stake in the struggle between Stilicho and Rufinus. Stilicho, of whom Claudian gives a most attractive portrait, while utterly damning Rufinus,[1] took the field against Alaric, who had severed his allegiance to Rome, and could have liquidated the Gothic menace in 396, but for the jealousy of Rufinus, who ordered him out of Greece. Stilicho's answer to that piece of arrogance was the murder of Rufinus. In 397 Stilicho again defeated Alaric, near Elis, but immediately afterwards we find Alaric being "appeased" by being appointed commander-in-chief of the Roman army in Illyricum! Perhaps the troubles in Africa were responsible at least in part for this soft policy. There, a sinister Moor called Gildo, who had for the past ten or twelve years been in command of the Roman garrison, rebelled, and by holding up the corn fleet, would have reduced Rome to famine, had not Stilicho promptly despatched Gildo's own brother Mascezel to crush him.[2] He succeeded, but Stilicho nevertheless had him executed that same year.

Yet a third time did Stilicho clash with Alaric, who had once again turned against Rome and invaded Italy, at Pollentia in 402. We do not know where Alaric spent the next few years. In 405 yet another barbarian chief, Radagaisus, swept into Italy with a horde of Germans, spreading panic and ruin far and wide. Stilicho defeated him in the following year, near Florence, whereupon 12,000 of the tribesmen were enlisted in the Roman army.

The end was now near. On the last night of the year 406 there occurred the great break-through. A vast agglomeration of Alans, Vandals, Suevians and Burgundians forced their way across the Rhine defences and descended on Gaul; while Britain, as usual, produced its own crop of pretenders. Alaric saw his chance. He decided to use blackmail this time. He claimed that having as a Roman general occupied Epirus, according to orders, he had been deserted and let down, and was therefore entitled to 4,000 pounds of gold as compensation.

---

[1] Notably in his long poems *Against Rufinus* and *On Stilicho's Consulship*.

[2] By this period, the Egyptian harvest was the source of Constantinople's food supply, that of Africa being earmarked for Rome.

As Jones[1] points out, the demand was outrageous, 4,000 pounds of gold being the annual income of a wealthy senator. Nevertheless, to keep Alaric at least neutral at this awful juncture, the money must be paid, and paid it was.

Stilicho, the one man who had shewn himself a match for Alaric, was executed in 408 at the instigation of a vile courtier called Olympius. The Roman troops, who had long been jealous of the tribal federate formations, now decided to massacre them, whereupon 30,000 of the federates went off to join Alaric. Alaric still tried to come to terms: he asked apparently for a much smaller sum of money this time, and for leave to settle his homeless and hungry tribe in Pannonia. The same intriguing chamberlain, Olympius, as had secured Stilicho's death, now advised Honorius who was at Ravenna, to reject Alaric's demand. Alaric at once moved south and blockaded Rome. For the second time he was bought off by the senate, who on this occasion paid 5,000 pounds of gold, 30,000 of silver, various other gifts and 3,000 of pepper.[2] But Alaric made it a condition that the senate persuade the emperor to accept him as an ally once again. Two delegations went from Rome to Ravenna to urge this course on Honorius. Olympius frustrated their efforts, but took only half-hearted steps to compel Alaric to retire. Ataulf was thus able to bring up reinforcements.

Olympius had by this time been suppressed, and his successor Jovian decided to come to terms. Alaric now demanded gold, corn and the right to settle his homeless people in the lands at the north end of the Adriatic sea. Jovian recommended that Honorius appoint Alaric commander-in-chief. This may seem surprising; but it must be remembered that all along Alaric had made it clear that his chief aim was to be able to settle and to feed his tribe within the pale of the empire – as so many others had done before him. Honorius, who had absolutely no competent troops to rely on, rejected the request in insulting language, which Jovian tactlessly read aloud to Alaric. For the second time, Alaric marched on Rome. Here he heard the alarming news that Honorius, for lack of Romans, had enlisted the help of 10,000 Huns – the most deadly enemy of both Roman and Goth. (Could the honour of Rome fall lower?) Alaric therefore was content to ask only for some corn, no

---

[1] p. 185.

[2] A precious commodity in antiquity. As late as the seventeenth century, an English King could finance an army on pepper.

gold and two portions of Noricum, which were largely unin-
habited and waste. Jovian refused the request. Alaric now
induced the senate, under the threat of starvation, to disregard
Honorius and to elect as emperor the prefect of the city,
Attalus, whose first act was to confer on Alaric the coveted
office of commander-in-chief. But no good came of it for
Alaric. Honorius received more troops from the east, and
Alaric's attempt to gain control of Africa failed. Alaric, at
his wits' end, now tried to come to terms with Honorius by
dethroning his own creature, Attalus. Alaric and Honorius
met near Ravenna; but the interview produced no solution,
and Alaric was goaded to anger by the presence of one of his
own chieftains who had defected to the Romans.

For the third time, this bewildered, homeless northerner,
rejected and rebuffed by the very Rome he had courted for
so long, approached her ramparts. But this time there was no
parleying: he assaulted, took and sacked the city.

CHAPTER VI

"Eleven hundred and sixty-three years after the foundation of Rome, the Imperial city, which had subdued and civilized so considerable a part of mankind, was delivered to the licentious fury of the tribes of Germany and Scythia." Thus does Gibbon[1] sum up in a phrase the events of 24th to 26th August, A.D. 410. In all the long history of Rome, no single occurrence is more difficult to evaluate, as regards both fact and effect.

Alaric was no savage. He was a tribal king, in search of a home and a living for his tribe. There were plenty of precedents for the settlement of outlanders within the Roman frontier. Had Stilicho been alive, matters might well have been "realistically" settled, as indeed there were to be several future opportunities of their being; but in each case the trembling obstinacy of Honorius, isolated and etiolated amid the miasmas of Ravenna, prevented any rational and radical solution. Alaric was thus compelled to turn from blackmail to violence. For Alaric himself, the capture of Rome was an empty triumph. What Alaric wanted was food, and the city was starving. That beyond doubt is why he dwelt there only three days, before setting out for the strait of Messina, whence he hoped to invade Africa and help himself to its magazines of grain. Adverse winds having scattered his fleet, Alaric in despair turned north once again, and died before the end of the year.

During the three days the sack lasted, enormous quantities of portable loot were carried off; but a looter can carry no more than any other kind of porter, nor, without a fleet or a transport train, can he carry it very far. Gibbon refers to the "waggons that always followed the march of a Gothic army", as the receptacles of the pillaged treasures; but in the prevailing famine which must have enfeebled beasts no less than men it is doubtful whether even these could have accommodated a freight so far in excess of their usual burdens. On the analogy of the Low Countries and of Spain, whose fairest towns have

[1] Chap. XXXI.

again and again been the victims of military robbery,[1] and are
yet to-day among the cynosures of Europe, it would be im-
prudent to exaggerate the material damage done by Alaric's
40,000 to the Eternal City. Indeed, the one surely ascertained
fact in this connexion is that enough was left to provide
Gaiseric[2] with a far richer and more disastrous booty. As
Gibbon was the first to point out, Alaric's visitation was mild
in comparison with that of the troops of Charles V in 1527,
when the city was abandoned to the rapacious insolence of his
northern mercenaries not for three days but for nine months.

Turning from the material to the human, we are at once
impressed by Alaric's clemency. He was an Arian Christian,
as were most of his followers, and he accordingly gave strict
orders that blood must not be shed, nor virtue invaded, and
that the shrines of the holy apostles must be respected. That
murders were committed, and lust slaked, is not to be denied;
but the majority of such crimes were committed not by Alaric
and his men but by slaves, who took the opportunity afforded
by anarchy to revenge themselves on their haughty masters
and mistresses – an ugly commentary on the basic putrescence
of Roman society.

The whole event is best contemplated through the eyes
of a man who was not only among the greatest of men then
living, but of those who have ever lived, a man who knew the
horrors of invasion, and was to die with the barbarians quite
literally at the door: St Augustine. In his *City of God*,[3] com-
paring the efficacy of pagan and Christian ideas of deity he
writes:

"There is an event of very recent date, within my own
memory, in which God acted miraculously and mercifully.
But the pagans do not remember the event with thanksgiving;
rather they attempt, as far as they can, to forget it. If I should
fail to mention it, I should be equally ungrateful. Radagaisus,[4] king of the Goths, with a huge and savage force had
now [A.D. 405] encamped in the neighbourhood of the city
and was threatening the Romans with the yoke of slavery.
But in one day he was so swiftly and thoroughly beaten that
while not a single Roman was killed, nor even wounded,

---

[1] It must be remembered that looting was regarded as a normal military
exercise, in accord with the accepted rules of warfare, until the Duke of
Wellington repressed it. Not even he was able to abolish it entirely. See
also the citation from St Augustine below.

[2] p. 87 below.   [3] V, xxxi.   [4] p. 53 above.

more than a hundred thousand of his army were laid low. He himself was soon captured and executed, as he deserved. For if that man, so ungodly, had entered Rome with such an army of ungodly troops, who would have been spared? What shrines of martyrs would he have respected? Before what person would he have shewn the fear of God? Whose blood would he have wished to see unshed? Whose modesty to see unravaged? And what shouts the pagans would have raised in favour of their gods, with what contumely would they have boasted! They would have said that he had conquered and displayed such power because he sought to please the gods with daily sacrifice, and summoned them to his side, a thing that the Christian religion did not allow the Romans to do.

"For as he was now approaching the scene where by the will of almighty God he was crushed, while the reports of his coming were spreading everywhere, we in Carthage were told that the pagans believed this and broadcast it boastfully. They said that, with the help and protection of the friendly gods to whom he made daily sacrifice, he could not possibly be defeated by men who offered no such sacrifices to the Roman gods, and allowed no one to make them. Nor do they now, poor wretches, thank God for his great mercy. For although he had determined to punish with a barbarian invasion the immorality of men who deserved to suffer worse, he tempered his indignation with great mercies. First he brought about the miraculous defeat of Radagaisus, lest the glory of victory should be conferred on the demons whom he was known to worship. Then he allowed Rome to be captured by these other barbarians, who, *contrary to the customs of all wars waged before*, spared those who fled to holy places out of reverence for the name of Christ. Moreover, they attacked in the name of Christ the very demons and rites of unholy sacrifice on which Radagaisus had relied, with such vigour that they seemed to be waging a far more bitter war with gods than with men. Thus the true lord and ruler of the world scourged the Romans with his merciful rod and also showed by the incredible defeat of the worshippers of demons that their sacrifices are not necessary even for safety in this present world. Thus those who are not stubborn in argument, but give prudent attention to facts, will not desert the true religion on account of its present tribulations, but will rather hold fast to it in the sure expectation of eternal life."

The foregoing chapter has been quoted in its entirety, for

two reasons. The first is the proportion of its content which is given to the sack of Rome by Alaric (who is not even mentioned by name). The event is recorded, no more. There are no lamentations, no threnody. The second is that in the eyes of Augustine Alaric is the instrument of God, for the chastening of the godless Romans, and more humane than any former warrior.

If this was the view of a contemporary,[1] who lived within five hundred miles of Rome, why was it that to many others, both at that time and ever since, "the sack of Rome by Alaric" has been regarded as traumatically final, in a manner that the far worse pillage of Gaiseric never has been? Many indeed would be hard put to it to say who Gaiseric was or when he pillaged Rome, but Alaric is a household name.

For this three reasons may be assigned, the first fortuitous, the second circumstantial, the third cardinal.

One of the greatest of Augustine's contemporaries, of whom, as of Augustine, much will be said later, was a Roman expatriate living in Bethlehem in Palestine, Jerome by name. Augustine was an African by birth, the town of Tagaste being what he called his *carnalis patria*.[2] Augustine had known Rome briefly and unhappily as an ill-treated schoolmaster: Jerome had been caressed by its most influential society and had at one time been secretary to a pope. He had been living in Bethlehem for nearly thirty years, but was still a Roman at heart, with all the added nostalgia of "the heart untravelled". He was also enormously influential. The range of his correspondents was as wide as that of the Latin-speaking world. It follows therefore that any pronouncement by Jerome on any subject would make a deep impression. It did.

Two years after Alaric's capture of Rome he is writing to an official of high rank, serving in Africa, who had asked for guidance on the question of the origin of the soul. In the course of his reply,[3] after bidding the family consult their bishop Augustine who is "both learned and holy", he says:

"I have long wished to get down to the prophecies of Ezekiel, and make good the promises which I have so often given to curious readers. When, however, I began to dictate

---

[1] It is supported by others. "Orosius and Olympiodorus, who are excellent contemporary authorities, both remark on the prosperity of Rome in the years which followed on the sack of 410." Ernest Barker, in Ch. xvi, p. 399, of *Cambridge Medieval History*.

[2] *Ep.* CXXIV.

[3] *Letter* CXXVI, 2.

I was so confounded by the havoc wrought in the west, and above all by the sack of Rome that, as the saying goes, I forgot my own name. 'Long did I remain silent knowing that it was a time to weep.'[1] This year I began again and had written three books of commentary when a sudden incursion of those barbarians of whom your Virgil speaks as the 'far-wandering men of Barce'[2] and to whom may be applied what holy scripture says of Ishmael, 'he shall dwell over against all his brethren'[3] overran the borders of Egypt, Palestine, Phoenicia and Syria, and like a raging torrent carried everything before them. It was with difficulty and only through the mercy of Christ that we were able to escape from their hands. But if as the great orator says 'amid the clash of arms law ceases to be heard'[4] how much more truly may it be said that war puts an end to the study of holy scriptures?''

What a difference from the unstudied flow of Augustine: two quotations from scripture, one from Virgil and one from Cicero. The Virgil one does not even fit, because Barce is in Cyrenaica, and the Bedu who had overrun the Levant were those of the Syrian desert, who swooped on their prey like kites and made off with it.

In another letter[5] addressed in the same year to a Roman lady Jerome writes:

"Whilst these things were happening in Jebus [i.e. Jerusalem] a dreadful rumour came from the west. Rome had been besieged [in 408] and its citizens had been forced to buy their lives with gold. Then thus despoiled they had been besieged again so as to lose not their substance only but their lives. My voice sticks in my throat; and as I dictate, sobs choke my utterance. The City which had taken the whole world was itself taken; nay more, famine was beforehand with the sword and but few citizens were left to be made captives. In their frenzy the people had recourse to hideous food; and tore each other limb from limb that they might have flesh to eat. Even the mother did not spare the babe at her breast. In the night was Moab taken, in the night did her wall fall down.[6] 'O God the heathen have come into thine inheritance; thy holy temple have they defiled; they have made Jerusalem an orchard. The

[1] *Eccl.* III, 4.
[2] *Aeneid* IV, 43.
[3] *Gen.* XVI, 12, R. V. marg.
[4] Cicero, *Pro Milone*, 4.
[5] CXXVII.
[6] *Isa.* XV, 1.

dead bodies of thy servants they have given to be meat unto the fowls of the heaven, the flesh of thy saints unto the beasts of the earth. Their blood have they shed round about Jerusalem; and there was none to bury them.'[1] 'Who could unfold in speech that night's havoc? Who its carnage? Or who could match our toils with tears? The ancient city falls, for many years a queen; in heaps lifeless corpses lie scattered amid the streets, amid the homes and hallowed portals of the gods. Everywhere is cruel grief, everywhere panic, and full many a shape of death.'[2] "

Moab, Jerusalem, Troy – all are summoned to suggest the fate of Rome. It can be imagined what an effect this ardent rhetoric would have, backed by the unique prestige of its writer. Ladies and gentlemen to whom this letter would be read with pride might be excused for supposing that what Virgil imagines to have happened in Troy a thousand years before actually had happened in Rome two years before. The continuation of the letter is therefore of all the greater interest. Jerome goes straight on:

"Meantime, as was natural in a scene of such confusion, one of the bloodstained victors found his way into Marcella's house. Suffer me to tell what I have heard,[3] to relate what holy men have seen; for there were some such present, and they say that you too were with her in the hour of danger.[4] When the soldiers entered she is said to have received them without any look of alarm; and when they asked her for gold she pointed to her coarse dress to shew them she had no buried treasure. However, they would not believe in her self-chosen poverty, but scourged her and beat her with cudgels. She is said to have felt no pain but to have thrown herself at their feet and to have pleaded with tears for you, that you might not be taken from her, or owing to your youth have to endure what she as an old woman had no occasion to fear. Christ softened their hard hearts, and even among bloodstained swords natural affection asserted its rights. The barbarians conveyed both you and her to the basilica of the apostle Paul,[5]

[1] Psalm LXXIX.

[2] Virgil, *Aen.* II, 361.

[3] Virgil again – *Aen.* VI, 266.

[4] The recipient of this letter, Principia, was Marcella's closest friend.

[5] St Paul without the Walls, built by Constantine, enlarged by Valentinian II and Theodosius and finished, ironically enough, by Honorius. Before the building of the existing St Peter's, it was the largest church in Rome, almost the same size as the basilica Ulpia in Trajan's forum.

that you might find there either a place of safety, or if not that at least a tomb. Hereupon Marcella is said to have burst into great joy and to have thanked God for having kept you unharmed in answer to her prayer. She said she was thankful too that the taking of the city had found her poor, not made her so, that she was now in want of daily bread, that Christ satisfied her needs so that she no longer felt hunger, that she was able to say in word and deed: 'naked came I out of my mother's womb, and naked shall I return thither: the Lord gave and the Lord hath taken away; blessed be the name of the Lord'.[1]" Here is an actual example of the clemency of Alaric's troops in obedience to Alaric's orders.

Orosius has a similar story – and Orosius was a contemporary, a pupil of Augustine. "While the barbarians were roaming about the city, it happened that one of the Goths, a man of authority and a Christian, came on an elderly virgin, dedicated to God, in a certain religious house. He asked politely for gold and silver, to which she replied in accordance with the precepts of her faith that she had quite a lot, and soon went to get it and handed it over. When the treasures were displayed, the barbarian was astonished at their weight, their size and their beauty: he had never seen anything like them before. Whereupon the virgin said to him: 'These are the sacred vessels of the apostle Peter. Take, if you dare, what you see. I'm not strong enough to defend them, so I dare not keep them.' The barbarian, overcome by reverence for religion, the fear of God and the faith of the virgin, sent a messenger to Alaric to tell him about the matter. Alaric ordered that all the sacred vessels should at once be taken back to the basilica of the apostle, and that the virgin and all the Christians in her household should be escorted there with the same immunity. The house, they say, was some way from the sacred buildings, and half the city lay between. So a great procession was formed, the people going one by one, with the gold and silver held high above their heads, defended on all sides by drawn swords. Thus the holy pageant was bedecked. Romans and barbarians together sang hymns to God; and the trumpet rang out to sound a truce, and to summon all those who were in hiding. From every side people ran to the vessels of Peter, the vessels of Christ. Many pagans, too, joined with the Christians in professing the faith, even though they did not hold it, and by that ruse escaped for the time being. And the greater became the

[1] *Job* I, 21.

flood of fugitives, the more eager were the barbarians to rally round them and defend them."[1]

Next year, 413, Jerome is still writing in the same vein. His friend Gaudentius had written from Rome to consult Jerome on how to bring up his daughter, whom he had dedicated while still an infant to a life of virginity. In the course of Jerome's reply occurs the following paragraph:

"The world sinks into ruin: yes, but shameful to say our sins still live and flourish. The renowned city, the capital of the Roman empire, is swallowed up in one tremendous fire; and there is no part of the earth where Romans are not in exile."

And that brings us to the second of the three reasons mentioned above, namely the refugees.

At the first approach of Alaric the exodus of Rome's citizens had begun. The parallel with our own age is here painfully close. Those who went soonest fared best. Many of them were poor folk, artisans, shipmen and such, who found a refuge in Africa. It is a sign of the times that as soon as a semblance of order was restored, instructions were sent to the governor of the province that these wretched creatures were to be rounded up and returned to the capital, there to resume their servile and indispensable drudgery. Some succeeded in reaching Constantinople, or even, such was Jerome's fame, Bethlehem. In his work on Ezekiel Jerome writes:[2]

"Who would believe that Rome, built up by the conquest of the whole world, had collapsed, that the mother of nations had become also their tomb? That the shores of the whole east, of Egypt, of Africa, which once belonged to the imperial city, were filled with the hosts of her men-servants and maid-servants; that we should every day be receiving in this holy Bethlehem men and women who were once noble and abounding in wealth, but are now reduced to poverty? We cannot relieve these sufferers: all we can do is to sympathize with them, and unite our tears with theirs."

And later[3] when relief was evidently better organized:

"There is not a single hour, nor a single moment, in which we are not relieving crowds of brethren, and the quiet of the monastery has been changed into the bustle of a guest house. And so much is this the case that we must either close our doors, or abandon the study of the Scriptures on which we

---

[1] Orosius, *Adversus Paganos*, Book VII, c. 39.
[2] Preface to Book III.   [3] Preface to Book VII.

depend for keeping the doors open. And so turning to profit, or rather stealing, the hours of the nights, which, now that winter is approaching, begin to lengthen somewhat, I am trying by the light of the lamp to dictate these comments whatever they may be worth, and am trying to mitigate with exposition the weariness of a mind which is a stranger to rest. I am not boasting, as some perhaps suspect, of the welcome given to the brethren, but I am simply confessing the causes of the delay. Who could boast, when the flight of the people of the west, and the holy places crowded as they are with penniless fugitives, naked and wounded, reveal the ravages of the barbarians? We cannot see what has occurred without tears and moans. Who would have believed that mighty Rome with its careless security of wealth would be reduced to such extremities as to need shelter, food and clothing? And yet some are so hard-hearted and cruel that instead of shewing compassion, they tear up the rags and bundles of the captives, and expect to find gold about those who are nothing but prisoners."[1]

There were it is true a few favoured nobles of Rome who simply retired to their vast estates in Africa.[2] But the generality of the refugees were as Jerome describes them. It is not hard to imagine the daunting, menacing, doom-laden sense of loss and foreboding that these poor people, unwitting and unwilling prophets and publishers of disaster must have spread throughout the whole empire.

And that brings us to the third reason why "410" carries even to-day so dread an overtone. It was the appalling inconceivability of the disaster. The idea that Rome could fall was preposterous.

A century before, Lactantius, who from the beauty of his style became known as the Christian Cicero, had written:[3]

"However much the authorities disagree, the end [of the world] is evidently expected to come in not more than two hundred years. It is obvious that the actual fall of things must

---

[1] It is to be noted that when Jerome is describing his own first-hand experiences he writes as a warm-hearted saint. The rhetoric and the quotations are laid aside.

[2] Among them was a pious lady called Melania, who settled in Augustine's birth-place, Tagaste. She there acquired an estate larger than the town itself. It contained not only many workers but a bath and two bishops as well – one Catholic, one heretic. She presented the whole estate to the church at Tagaste. See note on p. 219 of *St Augustine, Select Letters,* Loeb edn.

[3] *Divine Institutions, VII,* 25.

come fairly soon, except that so long as Rome stands nothing of the sort need be feared. But when that head of the world has fallen, and the downward rush begins, as the Sybil foretells, who would doubt that an end had come to human affairs and the world in general? It is the state that hitherto sustains everything."

Ammianus, five decades later, had declared:[1] "At the time when Rome first began to rise into a position of world-wide splendour, destined to live so long as men shall exist, in order that she might grow to a towering stature, Virtue and Fortune, ordinarily at variance, formed a pact of eternal peace." Only a few years before 410 the poet Claudian had written: "Nor will there ever be a limit to the empire of Rome."

And now the unimaginable had happened. The occupation of a national capital always leaves a wound, even when the invader has been driven out and the healing balm of victory has been applied.[2] But in 410 men had the dread prescience that, even though Rome might live at peace for a little longer, what had happened once might happen again, that, to use the chilling phrase of nuclear strategists, the rest of Rome's life would be but a "broken-backed war". And they were right.

The real significance of the year 410 is neither material, nor physical, nor political: it is spiritual, and of all ills, spiritual ills are the hardest to bear, the least easy to cure.

[1] XIV, 6, 3.
[2] Paris, Berlin, Tokyo – how many more examples has our own age shewn? 1814 seems a long time ago, but the British occupation of Washington still rankles in American breasts.

CHAPTER VII

THE BIRTH OF EUROPE

The fifth century had begun with disaster for Rome: it was to end in the emergence of Europe. No single century, before or since, has seen so radical and permanent a transformation in the ethnic and political disposition of the European continent.

After 410 the old life seemed to have been restored. Fugitives returned, government was resumed. Rutilius Namatianus, a rich nobleman from Gaul who had been prefect of the city, in the poem which describes his return home only six years later, while admitting that he has to travel by sea because the Goths have devastated the land and broken the bridges, could nevertheless laud Rome as though she were still what she had always been. "Fairest queen of the world, mother of men and mother of gods,"[1] he calls her. The sun-god who holds all together revolves only for her.[2] *"Urbem fecisti quod prius orbis erat"*: "You have made a city of what before was a world."[3] That Rome rules is a lesser thing than that she deserves to rule.[4] Yes, all would be well. The Gauls, Hannibal – Rome had risen superior to both. Rome is immortal, and "the span which remains has no bounds, so long as earth shall stand and heaven uphold the stars".[5] "That will regenerate thee which has ended other realms: the scheme of rebirth is to be able to grow by disasters."[6]

The facts of history were to be very different. Before an attempt is made to unravel the extremely complex and diffuse process of dissolution as it affected Italy, Spain, Africa, Illyria, Gaul and Britain, it may be helpful to present the contrast of what that area (the greater part of the western part of the empire) was at the end of the century, compared with its almost homogeneous unity at the beginning.

When, under pressure from the Huns, the great break-through occurred on the Rhine in 406, the catastrophe was started: within twenty-five years Italy was surrounded by barbarian kingdoms in Gaul, Italy, Spain and Africa. The struggle was hopeless. By the end of the century Italy, after being ruled

[1] 1, 49.   [2] 57.   [3] 66.   [4] 91.   [5] 136.   [6] 139–40.

by Odovacer, a Rugian from beyond the Danube who had, with contemptuous clemency, banished the last of the Caesars, formed part of the kingdom of the Ostrogoth, Theodoric with most of Illyria as his appanage. To the north, the Burgundians were established in what is now western Switzerland and the Lyonnais. To the north of them again we find the king of the Franks, Clovis, who would ere long establish his other frontiers as the Loire, the Black Forest and the English Channel with Troyes and Basel as his most southern cities. In Britain the Angles, Saxons and Jutes had subdued the Britons, some of whom still cringed in the far west of their island, while others had emigrated to what is now called Brittany in the north-west of France. France south of the Loire, including Toulouse, Narbonne and Marseilles and nearly the whole of Spain, made up the kingdom of the Visigoths, with the Sueves and Cantabrians perched in the northern extremity of the peninsula. Roman Africa, with Sicily and Sardinia, was ruled by the Vandals, who had, in addition, become a formidable maritime power. (See Map 2.) In short, by the dawn of the sixth century Europe, the multi-racial continent we still know, had replaced the empire. The various successor states, moreover, regarded themselves as in very varying degrees still as in some "special relationship" with Rome. Some claimed to be its allies to be appointed by the emperor in Byzantium, even when they had suppressed his western colleague, others regarded themselves, and were regarded by Rome, as being *foederati*, allies settled within the frontier. Others again were directly hostile.

There is a morbid parallel here with the state of disunited and sometimes inharmonious association, if such it can be called, between the successor states which come into being when a great colonial empire dissolves or is torn apart in our own day: just as the word Empire meant different things to different men, even so does the word Commonwealth: to some it is a vital and cherished reality, to some a convenience, to others a word only. The process is the same: it was only that Europe started it fifteen centuries before Africa and Asia.

But history never repeats itself, and there is one cardinal difference between the emergence of modern states and those of which we are treating. Modern states, to become such, merely alter their status, ethnically and culturally they remain the same. Their populations have been settled in their present abodes for centuries, millennia sometimes. What makes the fifth century so confused is that every single one of the new

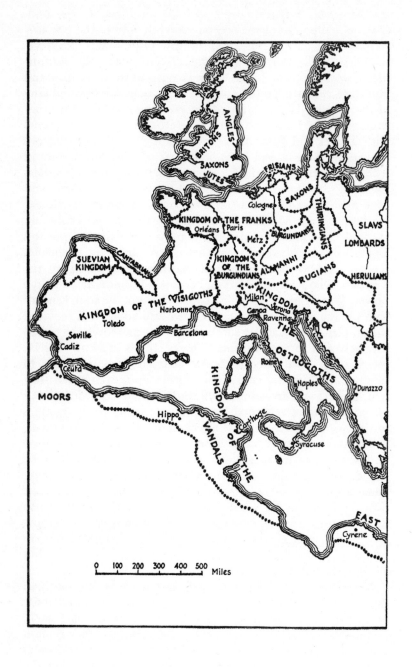

ANGLES

BRITONS

SAXONS
JUTES

FRISIANS

SAXONS

THURINGIANS

SLAVS

Cologne

KINGDOM OF THE FRANKS
Orléans   Paris

BURGUNDIANS

LOMBARDS

SUEVIAN
KINGDOM

CANTABRIANS

Metz

KINGDOM
OF THE
BURGUNDIANS

ALAMANNI

RUGIANS

HERULIANS

KINGDOM OF THE VISIGOTHS

Toledo

Narbonne

Milan   Verona

KINGDOM

Genoa
Ravenna

OF

Seville

Cadiz

Barcelona

THE

Ceuta

Rome

OSTROGOTHS

MOORS

Hippo

Carthage

Naples

Durazzo

KINGDOM

OF   THE

Syracuse

VANDALS

EAST

Cyrene

0   100   200   300   400   500   Miles

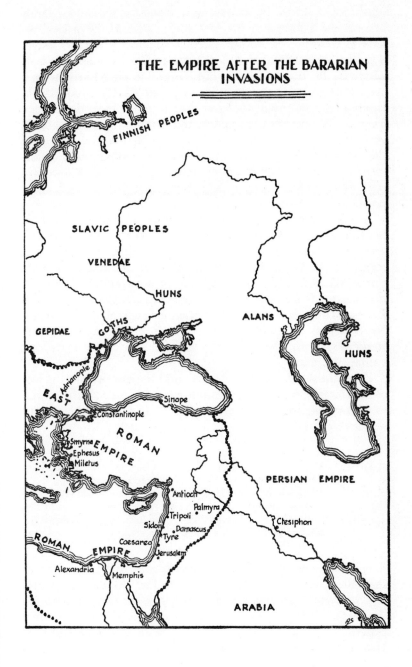

THE EMPIRE AFTER THE BARARIAN
INVASIONS

states was erected by newcomers, from the unknown lands beyond the Rhine and the Danube. Thus, in the period we have to consider, the dominant external factor is the successive, tide-like, occupation of region after region by outlanders, of whom by far the greatest is the Visigothic king Euric, who is even able to unite the enemies of Rome for the final attack. Internally, a more surprising evolution takes place, the change from the autocracy of Diocletian and Constantine to something very like a constitutional monarchy, with the last *epigoni* of the Theodosian dynasty, "transient and embarrassed phantoms", ruled by commanders-in-chief, most of whom are barbarians, with a surprising rejuvenescense of senatorial power and prestige.

In earlier epochs of the Roman republic and empire it is possible to view history from the centre, from the City: everything turns on Rome, and on Rome's rulers. But now the scene has become bewilderingly diffuse: no longer can we survey the world from the Palatine or the Capitol. We must investigate Ravenna, visit Milan, evaluate and compare Lyons, Toulouse, Barcelona, Richborough and Carthage. Nevertheless, we shall get quite lost in this maze unless we stand above its alleys, at the centre, and make Italy our vantage-point.

From the death of Alaric in 410, and the dismissal of the last of the Caesars, poor little Romulus Augustus, in 476, the march of history progresses in three stages.[1] It may be helpful to set them out in tabular form:

		Rome	*Provinces*
1.	410–423	Patriciate of Constantius to death of Honorius.	Visigoths settle in southern France.
2.	23–455	Patriciate of Aëtius, reign of Valentinian III.	Vandals settle in Africa. Huns invade Gaul and Italy.
3.	455–476	Patriciate of Ricimer. Extinction of Theodosian house in west.[2]	Odovacer settles in Italy, as king.

1. When towards the end of the year 410 Alaric died, he was succeeded as king by his brother-in-law Ataulf. If Alaric was a great national leader, Ataulf was an international innovator equally great, and more original. From his own experience, he had seen how great, how tough Rome still was. Indeed, men were already saying, now that they had recovered

[1] *Cambridge Medieval History*, Vol. 1, p. 399.
[2] See Appendix I.

from the shock of violation, that recent as the sack had been, men would think, as they beheld the multitude of the Roman people, and heard them talk, that nothing had happened, were it not for some traces of fire.[1] Ataulf therefore decided that, instead of opposing Rome, instead of being for ever ground to powder between the upper millstone of the Huns and the nether one of the empire, it would be more prudent to ally his people with them, indeed to coalesce with them, and so to face in unity the real enemy of both. Thus Ataulf, like Alexander of Macedon before him, saw himself as the pioneer of a society based on fusion, not fission. Neither lived to see his ideal state realized: but whereas the Graeco-Persian state never at any time came into being, the Romano-Gothic one eventually did. Ataulf must therefore be reckoned as one of the progenitors of the Holy Roman Empire, and hence of modern Europe itself. He had one great asset: Galla Placidia, the sister of Honorius. He married her with great pomp at Narbonne.[2] Orosius tells us[3] that once when he was in Beth-lehem, visiting St Jerome, he met a man who had been a close friend of Ataulf and had attended his wedding. He was, says Orosius, a religious-minded and prudent official, who had often heard Ataulf describe his theory of government thus: "Originally he had ardently desired to wipe out the Roman name, and to make the whole of the Roman realm an empire of the Goths, and to call it so: it was to be, if I may use a colloquialism, *Gothia*, instead of *Romania*: Ataulf was to be what Caesar Augustus had been. But from long experience he found that the Goths were incapable of obeying laws, owing to their unbridled wildness, and that without respect for laws it was quite impossible to found a stable state. So he decided to declare in favour of sustaining the Roman empire, and acting in the Roman name by the strength of the Goths, and thus to win from posterity the title of restorer, since he could not acquire that of substitute. He therefore did all in his power to abstain from war and to ensue peace."

But Ataulf, like Alaric before him, was to be frustrated and alienated by Honorius' myopic obstinacy. The actual sequence

---

[1] Orosius, *Adversus Paganos*, Book VII, c. 40. Another reliable contemporary, Olympiodorus, writing about a decade later, bears witness to the splendour of Rome: "The city is one house: the Urbs contains a myriad cities." The baths of Caracalla and Diocletian merit special mention. Frag. 43 (ed. Muller).

[2] See below, p. 73.　　　[3] *Ibid.*, c. 43.

of events is confused. Both Gaul and Spain became the victims
of what Orosius calls a "catalogue of tyrants", who raged like
Bacchanals through province after province.[1] But in 411 a
true Roman became commander-in-chief in the interests of
his legitimate master, Honorius. His name was Constantius,
born, like Constantine the Great, at Nish, but of no relationship
to him. He had, men said, as he rode along, the aspect of a
born ruler.[2] He was at once successful: he defeated one usurper,
called Gerontius, and captured another, called Constantine,
and sent him to Rome for execution. Meanwhile the Franks,
Alemanni and Burgundians had created yet another bogus
emperor, called Jovinus. It might have been thought that
Ataulf, when in the spring of 412 he entered Gaul, somewhere
near Valence, would have supported Jovinus against Honorius,
who had snubbed and slighted him. It would have given him
a region of southern Gaul to settle in – the goal of Frankish
policy for so long. The wretched puppet-emperor whom
Alaric had created, or forced the senate to create during his
parleys, Attalus, was still in Ataulf's train – a creature who in
Orosius's contemptuous phrase had been "made, unmade,
remade and de-made 'emperor'"[3] and he counselled collabora-
tion with Jovinus. Ataulf was playing for higher stakes: he
still hoped that somehow he could conciliate Honorius and so
become the heir of the childless emperor *jure uxoris*. In 413,
therefore, after parleys with the loyal prefect of the Gauls,
a treaty was made whereby Ataulf was to send Honorius the
heads of Jovinus and his brother, in return for regular food
supplies and the recognition of Ataulf's position in Bordeaux
and probably Aquitaine as well. The heads duly arrived in
Ravenna; but no food went north. This, it must be confessed,
was not wholly Honorius' fault. The Count of Africa, Heraclian, unfortunately decided that this was the psychological
moment for him, too, to revolt. He therefore withheld the
African grain shipments, and even invaded Italy. He was
defeated, returned to Africa and was assassinated at Carthage.
He had failed, but he had contributed his share to the ultimate
failure of Ataulf and his policy, because Ataulf, like his brother-
in-law, saw himself now compelled to seek by war what he
had failed to obtain by peace.

In the autumn of 413 Ataulf seized Toulouse and occupied
Narbonne. Marseilles held out against him, under the

[1] *Ibid.*, c. 42.   [2] Olympiodorus, frag. 23.
[3] *Ibid., imperatore facto, infecto, refecto ac defecto.*

leadership of Count Boniface, who was later to see the ruin of Africa.[1] It was at Narbonne, in January, 414, that he took the personally gratifying and politically irrevocable step of marrying Galla Placidia. The wedding was celebrated in the house of the principal citizen of the town. Both bride and bridegroom were clad after the Roman fashion. "Among other wedding-presents," Olympiodorus tells us,[2] "Ataulf presented his bride with fifty handsome boys, clothed in silk, each one carrying in either hand a large bowl, of which one was full of gold, the other of precious, or rather priceless, stones, which had formed part of the loot when Rome was sacked. Epithalamiums were sung, Attalus being the first performer, then Rusticus and Phoebadius. The whole ceremony gave the greatest joy and pleasure both to the barbarians and to the Romans who took part in it." At last the two races were one.

But at that very time Constantius, who had now become consul for the year, was inaugurating his entry into office with the usual games, which he paid for out of Heraclian's confiscated goods. In the spring he moved on Gaul. Here he found that Attalus was once again being used as a "front" by Ataulf, to maintain some shred of a link with the Roman name. He held court at Bordeaux. On the approach of Constantius, Ataulf set fire to the city, and was constrained to retreat to Barcelona in Spain. Clearly, with such strong forces arrayed against him, it was time to treat with Honorius. How much more urgent, and favourable, did negotiations appear to have been made by the birth of a son to Ataulf and Galla Placidia. The child was named Theodosius – a dynastic gesture. Attalus was again discarded: Ataulf would recognize Honorius, if Honorius would recognize Ataulf – and Theodosius. But the high and palmy Roman, Constantius, who had now been created *patricius* for his successes against the Goths, obstructed the plan: he had a higher and more palmy one. Then the little Theodosius died. He was buried in a silver coffin, while all Barcelona lamented. In that same city, in the autumn of 415, Ataulf was assassinated by a vindictive groom. Thus died Ataulf's great dream of uniting Gothic vigour with Roman blood. He was true to it to the end, and with his dying breath bade his brother send back Galla Placidia and make peace with Rome.

A boor called Sigerich succeeded Ataulf. He lasted only a

[1] pp. 78–9.
[2] Olympiodorus, Frag. 24; ed. Muller.

week, damned to memory by his brutality in making Galla
Placidia walk on foot for twelve miles in front of his horse.
The Goths then elected a certain Wallia, who looking back to
the great days of Alaric, decided on a hostile policy, and like
Alaric, planned to invade Africa. But although he was, in
Orosius' words,[1] "elected by the Goths to break the peace, he
was ordained by God to confirm it". His fleet was scattered
near Cadiz, and Wallia was forced to sue for terms. Rome
was now equally eager to come to them. In 416 the treaty
was made. In return for 600,000 measures of corn, Placidia
was restored to Rome.

And now comes the almost *Arabian Nights* end to the story.
In the following year, 417, Constantius became consul for the
second time, and married the reluctant Placidia. She bore him
two children, Honoria and Valentinian, and thus the question
of the succession was settled – but without any Gothic admix-
ture. If Placidia resented the way in which she had been
"redeemed", her countrymen were proud of her. And of
Constantius, too, who celebrated a triumph that same year.
It seemed as though peace had come again: Constantius had
recovered much of Gaul, Wallia was humbling the Vandals
and Alans in Spain.

In fact, Honorius had now done, ostensibly of his own
motion, what Alaric and Ataulf had urged him to do: he had
granted a settlement inside the Roman *limes* to a Teutonic
people living under its own king. In 418 Honorius issued a
constitution which gave Gaul local government, in which both
Romans and Goths were to share, both being represented at
the Council which had its seat at Arles, the Goths being
answerable, as federates, for the country's defence. "The
policy of decentralisation thus enunciated in 418," comments
Barker,[2] "and the combination of that policy with the settlement of the Visigoths in 419, indicate that the Empire was ceas-
ing to be centralised and Roman, and was becoming instead
Teutonic and local."

In 421 Honorius elevated Constantius, who had for a decade
been the real ruler of the west, to the dignity of Augustus, and
proclaimed him as his colleague. Placidia became Augusta,
too, at last. This led to a breach with Theodosius II, emperor
in the east, who refused to recognize his uncle Honorius'
action; but the speedy death of Constantius dissolved the risk
of war. Placidia now saw herself as the Empress Dowager, but

[1] *Op. cit.*, c. 43.   [2] *Cambridge Medieval History*, Vol. *cit.*, p. 405.

her overbearing interference alienated her brother, who banished her and the children to Constantinople. He died soon after, this poor, weak-minded man. He had lived "a stranger and afraid, in a world he never made". The world he left to posterity, too, was one he never made, and of which he neither willed nor understood the inevitable creation.

2. Coming now to the second of the epochs into which the first three quarters of the century were divided above, we enter a period which was to be dominated by two great events, the invasions of the Vandals and of the Huns. The stream of intrigue winds on its muddy course, cynics, adventurers and collaborators proliferate, Rome becomes ever less Roman – all these factors had been present for decades and would continue for many more, but they did not influence the ultimate outcome, the emergence of a new world. The Vandals and the Huns did: it is their conflicts with Rome which must now be reviewed.

To-day the mere names of Vandal and Hun carry overtones of chilling savagery which none of the other "barbarians" seem to stir; and yet in neither case does the modern conception coincide with ancient reality. The word "vandalism" is comparatively modern: it did not come into use until the end of the eighteenth century.[1] Just how brutal the Vandals – or for that matter any of the invaders – really were, it is not easy to gauge. "Atrocity" stories tend to be much the same in all ages; and we must discount much of what has come to us from such biased reporters as Victor of Vita, one of the leaders of the Catholic "resistance" movement in Africa. It is nevertheless clear from his circumstantial record that torture was used to elicit confessions of hidden wealth, that priests were used as beasts of burden, and that on at least one occasion at Bulla Regia, near Tunis, a Catholic congregation, while celebrating Easter, was shot to death by Arian arrows. On another occasion the minions of a certain Proculus tore up altar-linen to make shirts and drawers out of.[2] We know, too, from St Augustine, who lay on his death-bed in Hippo as the Vandals were battering on the city's gates, that they did treat the inhabitants of Africa with great savagery; and Augustine, as good a witness as any, only lived to experience the beginning of their conquest of Roman Africa.

[1] It appears to have been first used in its French form by Henri Grégoire bishop of Blois, c. 1793.
[2] *History of the Persecution of the Province of Africa*, Bk. I, 5, 41 and 39.

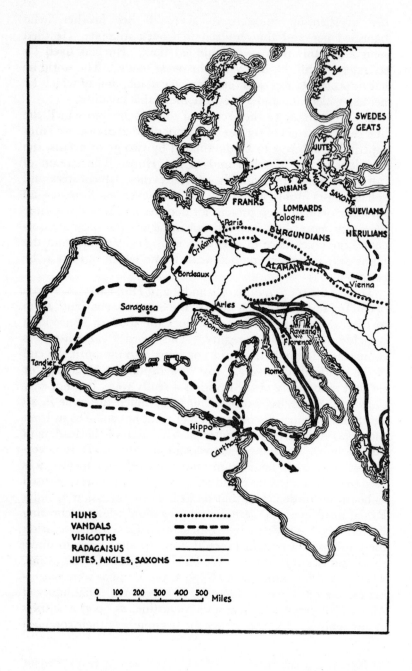

HUNS	••••••••••••
VANDALS	– – – – – –
VISIGOTHS	▬▬▬▬▬▬
RADAGAISUS	————
JUTES, ANGLES, SAXONS	–·–·–·–·–

0 100 200 300 400 500 Miles

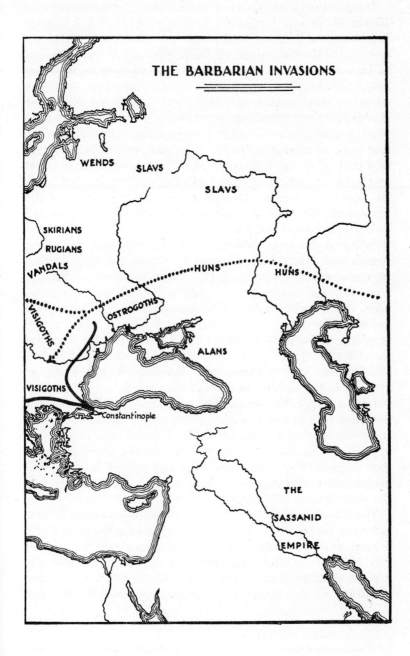

THE BARBARIAN INVASIONS

WENDS   SLAVS

SLAVS

SKIRIANS

RUGIANS

VANDALS

HUNS   HUNS

VISIGOTHS   OSTROGOTHS

ALANS

VISIGOTHS

Constantinople

THE

SASSANID

EMPIRE

It is hard to judge: if, in considering the incidents mentioned above, we deduct congenital human avarice, man's natural brutishness and Arian fanaticism, it is hard to isolate any specifically Vandal residue. Tacitus, who includes the Vandals in his catalogue of German tribes, describes them as being resourceful warriors, who even in his day knew how to inspire terror by night-attacks, in which they blacked out both their shields and their faces: "no enemy can face this novel and as it were hellish apparition: it is always the eyes that are the first to be overcome in battle".[1] Salvian, on the other hand, says that of all the barbarians the Vandals were the weakest and least formidable race; but Salvian, a fifth-century Christian, was an extremist who was apt to extol the virtues of the barbarians in order to castigate the sins of the Romans.[2] In drawing up a class-list of savagery, it is hard to know whom to place at the top. Probably our own ancestors, the Jutes, Angles and Saxons. They would have no truck with Rome;[3] on the contrary, they did all they could to obliterate Roman faith, law and language, together with many of the inhabitants. That is why in Britain the process of re-civilization, still unfinished in our own day, had to start all over again at the very end of the sixth century,[4] and why unlike the countries we still call "Latin", England has seldom succeeded in implanting her own manners and language in the souls, as opposed to the mouths, of races of alien stock.

In this respect the Angles and their accomplices resembled the Vandals and Huns: they are the only "barbarians" who, when the choice had to be made, rejected assimilation for opposition. In the event, both Vandals and Huns failed in their object. The name they have left behind is out of all proportion to anything they achieved; but had they succeeded, the whole history of Europe would have been different.

The Vandals were the first to try conclusions with Rome. After the great break-through they had swept down through France, to find a home in Spain. Just what made them move into Africa (as so often with the journeyings of the newcomers) it is not possible to say. One version has it that the governor of Africa, Count Boniface, the friend and backer of Galla

---

[1] *Germany*, 43.

[2] *De Gubernatione Dei*, VII, p. 64.

[3] This trait has survived to our own day in the Protestant underworld.

[4] It was in 596 that Augustine, prior of the Caelian monastery in Rome, received the orders of Pope Gregory to proceed to England.

Placidia, and the enemy of Aëtius, who tried to ruin his rival, invited the Vandals to come to his aid against the imperial forces. The story was widely believed and has done much to ruin Boniface's reputation. Another version has it that the Vandals were summoned to intervene by both sides. More natural causes more probably operated. The Vandals were being hard pressed by the Visigoths, who were soon to be the masters of almost the whole of Spain; and as the Romans had found from the days of Scipio to those of Hadrian, northern Africa is strategically linked with southern Spain. Exactly the same affinity in reverse was to draw the Muslim general Tarik to invade Spain in the year 711.[1]

The Vandals, led by Gaiseric, who had become king in the previous year, crossed the strait in 529, and as already related besieged and took Hippo in 530. Hippo became the first Vandal capital, the Romans retaining Carthage and Constantine. Technically the Vandals were federates of the emperor; but Gaiseric was set on independence and primacy. He had already beaten Boniface, who was soon afterwards recalled to Italy. He was, says Procopius,[2] not merely a skilled soldier but the cleverest of mankind. He at once set about assembling a fleet, with which he then raided Italy and Sicily. In 439 he suddenly seized Carthage, on 19th October, from which a new era was dated. Gaiseric made no pretence of being a Roman. On the contrary, his aim was to de-Romanize the province as thoroughly as possible. There was policy in this move, besides natural inclination. It must be remembered that all contemporary accounts of the occupation come from Catholic sources, whereas in Africa the heretical Donatists had for long been extremely strong and active. The Donatist heresy had originated in a difference of opinion as to how those who had bowed to the storm of persecution at the beginning of the fourth century should be treated. Donatus and his followers held that certain bishops were "traitors", because they had been willing to "hand over" (*tradere*) the sacred books to the imperial authorities. Rome, in the person of its bishop, took a more lenient view, but for that very reason – and this is the vital point – Donatism appealed, and appealed in increasingly violent and unchristian a form, to the latent Semitic nationalism of the Punic inhabitants of Africa. It became, in fact, a turbulent, secular and separatist movement. The Semites are among

---

[1] Thus giving us the name Gibraltar – *Jebel Tarik*, Tarik's hill.
[2] *Vandalic War*, III, iii, 24.

the toughest nationalists in all history. The Jews had proved
it again and again in their resistance to Rome, and so had the
Carthaginians before them. Both had been crushed, but in
both the germ of nationalism still lived. Augustine, himself
of African race, recognized this: he was adamant in his opposition to Donatism, but insisted that his clergy must be able to
address their flocks in the Punic vernacular. It was undoubtedly this spirit of Semitic separatism, this antagonism to the Greek
and Latin world, which made the inhabitants of North Africa
welcome so willingly and coalesce so easily with their Arab
Muslim brethren when they, in their turn, reasserted the dominance of Semitic faith and polity in the seventh century. Gaiseric, with his quicksilver wit, realized the latent hostility of
many of the North Africans to Rome, and determined to turn
it to good account. The fact that he and his men were Arians
provided another reason for opposing, and oppressing, the
Catholics.

From the secure harbours of Carthage and Hippo, Gaiseric's
warships operated on an ever-wider scale. Besides raiding
Sicily, Calabria and Campania, he extended his kingdom to
include Corsica, Sicily and Sardinia. By cutting off Rome's
corn supply, he sapped her strength, thereby succeeding where
Alaric and Ataulf had failed. In 455 Gaiseric and his horde
landed at Ostia and marched on Rome. For fourteen days,
as compared with Alaric's three, they looted it. They did far
more damage than the Goths, even stripping the gilded tiles
from the temple of Jupiter on the Capitol. Among the loot
they bore off to Carthage two items are of special interest.
The first was the empress Eudoxia and her daughters, who
would be valuable hostages in the case of a hostile move by
the empire. The other was the sacred vessels which Titus had
salvaged from the Temple in Jerusalem in the year 70, the
seven-branched lamp-stand, the table of the shewbread and
the trumpets, which to this day we behold graven on Titus'
triumphal arch in Rome.[1]

"Every year," says Procopius,[2] "at the beginning of spring,
Gaiseric invaded Sicily and Italy, enslaving some of the cities
and razing others to the ground, and plundering everything;

---

[1] They were recovered by Belisarius and taken to Constantinople, whence
at the instance of a pious Jew they were returned to Jerusalem, in time for
the Persian sack of 614. They have never been seen again. Procopius,
op. cit., IV, x, 5.

[2] *op. cit.*, III, v, 18–25.

and when the land had become destitute of either men or
money, he invaded the domain of the emperor of the east. So
he plundered Illyricum and most of the Peloponnese and the
rest of Greece and the adjacent islands. Then back he went to
Italy and Sicily, plundering and pillaging everywhere by
turns. One day he had embarked in his ship in the harbour
at Carthage, and the sails were already spread, when the
pilot, they say, asked him whom in all the world they were
to sail against. 'Evidently', he answered, 'against those with
whom God is angry.' "

The ravages of this Arian Cromwell would have been far
more devastating but for the heroism and ability of Aëtius, to
whom and to Boniface Procopius awards the title of "the last
of the Romans".[1] His father was a German from Pannonia,
his mother an Italian of noble birth. He understood the
barbarians. Just as Alaric and Attila had been hostages of
Rome, so Aëtius had been a hostage first of Alaric and then
of the Huns. But not even Aëtius could quell Gaiseric, who
was able to outwit both west and east, and to bring to nought
the armadas they despatched against him. Finally, in 476, he
did come to an understanding with the emperor Zeno, whereby
Gaiseric undertook to allow the Catholics freedom of worship,
restored Roman prisoners and allowed Roman slaves to be
redeemed. Zeno in return recognized the Vandal kingdom.
Gaiseric soon afterwards made over Sicily to Odovacer, who
would shortly be lord of Rome. Soon after, Gaiseric died.

His achievement had been spectacular. He and his 80,000[2]
had defied Rome and Constantinople, and had erected a
kingdom in one of the fairest and most fertile provinces of the
empire. Within a century, all was gone. Gaiseric's son,
Huneric, married Eudoxia, the elder of Valentinian's
daughters. (His previous wife, a child of the Visigoth king
Theodoric, he had repudiated, and sent her back to her father
without ears or nose.) But compared with his father, Huneric
was but a "Tumble-down Dick". The insidious delights of
Carthage and the valour of Belisarius did the rest. Within
the century the Vandal empire was extinct.

---

[1] III, iii, 15. The interest of the phrase lies less in those to whom it is
applied than in its being used at all: for Procopius, writing in the sixth
century, Rome and the Romans had ceased to be.

[2] Victor tells us – I, 2 – that before crossing the strait into Africa, Gaiseric
had held a census. The 80,000 included all his people, not only fighting
men.

By a historical irony, it was the Vandals, or rather Gaiseric, who gave to Europe one of its most stabilizing political principles, namely that of the succession to the crown being fixed in one family, and settled on the eldest surviving son of that family at the time of the king's decease, instead of being, as formerly, the prize to be snatched by the most powerful or unscrupulous of contending factions.[1] "The Vandal kingdom was the first and for a long time the only state in which the idea of a permanent rule of succession came to be realised – and rightly is Gaiseric's family statute reckoned in history among the most remarkable facts relating to public law."[2]

The Huns bequeathed nothing so valuable. In fact, they bequeathed nothing at all. They owe their retrospective reputation to one outstanding and extraordinary man, Attila, and to the fact that we have a more intimate picture of him and of his court than of any other barbarian chieftain. To start with, Ammianus has told us a good deal about the Huns,[3] of their unimaginable ferocity, their squat bodies, their great arms and shoulders, slit eyes and flat noses. Their cheeks were scarified in infancy to prevent the growth of hair. They ate raw flesh. They never changed their clothes. They stank. They lived all their days on horseback, their nights too, sleeping along the necks of their mounts. They were completely nomadic, these terrible little yellow men, and hauled their women and children behind them in wagons.

This description alone would be enough to set the Huns apart from other men, even barbarians, in popular estimation; but it so happens that we have an even closer view of Attila and his court on the Hungarian steppe, from the pen of a Greek with a Roman name, Priscus, who accompanied an embassy from the Byzantine court to Attila in the year 449. He has left us a narrative which in its detail, balance and colour recalls the best productions of the journalism of travel of the nineteenth century, when that form of literature was in its hey-day.[4] There is the long journey, the meeting with the envoys of the Huns, the first suspicious contacts, misunderstandings, explanations, resentments, the tactless remarks

---

[1] Victor, op. cit., II, 13; Procopius, History of the Wars, III, vii, 29. Gaiseric had himself obtained the throne through popular choice, the sons of his predecessor being disregarded.

[2] Barker, Cambridge Medieval History, Vol. I, p. 318.

[3] XXXI, ii, 1–12 seq.: see p. 52 above.

[4] Muller, Vol .IV, pp. 69 seq.

construed as insults – the scene has been re-enacted countless times when Europeans and Asians have assembled to discuss a possible accommodation. Then comes the long trek to Attila's court, secure beyond its five days' journey of scorched earth on the north bank of the Danube. The visitors wanted to pitch their tents *en route* on a hill, but that would have offended the majesty of their host, who assigned them a site on the plain where his own encampment was spread.

Attila's dwelling in Hungary was splendid. It was one great hall made of beautifully compacted wood, fenced round with a wooden palisade.[1] It was sumptuously furnished with rich carpets and tapestries. Gold, silks and gems abounded. There was a bath, on the Roman plan, supervised by a Greek. It was constructed of imported stone. There were banquets, at which the food was choice and the wine delicious. Minstrels and jesters entertained the guests during dinner, girls were there to solace them afterwards – a customary attention, says Priscus, which he modestly declined. Costly gifts were exchanged.

In the midst of all the splendour Attila sat stern, unsmiling and austere. While the guests ate off gold plates and drank from jewelled goblets, Attila ate frugally from a wooden platter and drank from a cup of the same material. "This man," says Jordanes,[2] "aspired to conquer the two greatest powers on earth, the Romans and the Visigoths. His army, they say, numbered half a million. He was born into this world in order to shake his own people, and to strike terror into everyone.[3] By some stroke of fate, the fear he inspired seemed to spread ahead of him. He had a proud gait, darting his eyes this way and that, and his pride of power shewed itself in the way he moved. He loved war, but kept a hold of himself when in action. He was an excellent councillor, and always accessible to petitioners, and kind to those he had received into his protection. He was short of stature, with a broad chest and a strong head. He had little eyes, a scanty beard streaked with gray, a snub nose and a darkish skin. In fact he was absolutely typical of his race."

[1] Dolgoruky's original Kremlin (1156) was also made of wood, and not until 1367 was it replaced by stone ramparts.

[2] c. xxxv.

[3] The figure given for his army is at least ten times too high. According to Amédée Thierry (*Histoire d'Attila*, Vol. II, p. 248), the expression "Attila Scourge of God" (*flagellum Dei*) occurs for the first time in the legend of St Loup, written in the eighth or ninth century by a priest of Troyes.

Except in one regard. For generations Huns had enlisted in the Roman army. Stilicho the Vandal had raised a whole regiment of them, so had Honorius.[1] Attila himself had served in the imperial forces; he also provided many recruits for the Roman army. Then, about the year 430, Attila realized that the empire was no longer a lion to be feared, but a cow to be milked.

He decided that he, not Rome, was to be master of the world. Like Alaric before him, he made his first essays against the eastern empire. His policy was simple: it was to alternate violence with blackmail. In the year 440 Rome was in sore straits. The year before, Carthage had fallen to the Vandals, which meant not only the loss of one of the empire's most abundant granaries but also that a hostile fleet based on Carthage could menace the eastern no less than the western dominions of Rome.

By a crippling coincidence, the Persians had chosen this very year to invade Roman Armenia, on what pretext is not known. The northern frontier was thus left almost bare. Attila saw that his chance had come, and decided to strike.

He crossed the Danube. Viminacium (modern Kostolacz), one of the major strong-points of the Roman *limes*, was captured and razed to the ground. So was Singidunum (Belgrade). Worst of all, Sirmium, the very key to the whole of the Danube defence system, fell to Attila. The Balkans lay open to him, but, content with his booty and his captives, he undertook no campaign in the following year. He preferred to treat with Rome. The Hun was now insistent that all of his tribesmen in Roman pay should be handed back to him – this demand was to recur in all his many negotiations with Rome. Henceforth, any Hun who took service in the Roman ranks was regarded as a traitor, who, if he were handed back, risked crucifixion or impalement. In 443 Attila renewed his offensive. Nish, the birth-place of Constantine, was captured and destroyed, and the Huns then swept down to the sea, which they reached at three different points. They approached Constantinople itself, but were too prudent to attack it. Nevertheless, Theodosius was forced to beg for terms. The barbarian exacted from the empire not only the return of the fugitives but arrears of tribute as well – Constantinople had been paying it for the past eight years – calculated at 6,000 pounds of gold. In addition, the sum payable under the treaty of 435 was to be trebled, which meant that

[1] P. 54 above.

Attila was to receive 2,000 pounds of gold each year. Roman prisoners who escaped from their Hun captors were to be ransomed at the rate of twelve *solidi* a head, in place of the eight formerly stipulated.

The embassy which arranged these humiliating provisions was followed by four more, in quick succession. Attila's object was simply to collect as often as possible the handsome presents which Theodosius felt constrained to give to his emissaries: he was as versatile in levying blackmail as he was resolute in war.

In 447 Attila again invaded the eastern empire, enfeebled once more by a series of destructive earthquakes, followed by plague. Not less than seventy towns were destroyed, and the invasion was checked only at Thermopylae. The next years were once again, in accordance with Attila's policy, devoted to negotiations, and it was in 449 that Priscus accompanied an embassy to Attila as already related. The same old subjects were discussed, the return of fugitives, the ransoming of prisoners; and a deputation from the west was there, too, to debate the apparently rather trivial matter of certain church plate from Sirmium, which Attila claimed was his by right of conquest, but which had in fact been taken to Rome and there pawned. The outcome we do not know.

Attila now decided that the time had come for him to turn against the west. One of the reasons he had hitherto held his hand was his friendship with Aëtius, the western commander-in-chief, who had been a hostage in the hands of the Huns as a boy, and still cultivated Attila's friendship. In fact, Attila was actually given the rank of *magister militum* of the western empire. It was not intended that he should command Roman troops; but the rank carried a good salary, and a liberal grain allowance. It was, in fact, a decorous and delicate instrument of bribery.

Attila's onslaught upon the west was to be launched through a woman. Galla Placidia had a daughter called Honoria. Like her mother, she was romantic. In the year 449 she was thirty-two, but alas! still unmarried. She allowed herself to be seduced by one of her gentlemen. The intrigue was discovered, the lover executed and Honoria engaged to a dull, rich senator. This was too much – or rather far too little – for Honoria. If her mother had married a barbarian king, why should not she? In the spring of 450 she sent a letter and a ring to Attila by a eunuch called Hyacinth, asking him, in return for a cash consideration, to rescue her from an impossible marriage.

Poor Honoria's plan was frustrated: Valentinian handed her over to Galla Placidia, who died soon afterwards, to be buried perhaps in the splendid tomb in Ravenna which she had done so little to deserve. What happened to Honoria we do not know; but Attila claimed her as his bride and half the western empire as her dowry. Gaiseric the Vandal, by far the subtlest manipulator of the century, urged him to press his claim.

In 451 Attila attacked. He crossed the Rhine, seized several French towns (though not as many as legend afterwards pretended) and on 23rd June had forced Orléans to surrender, when suddenly Aëtius appeared and put the besiegers to flight. At the head of his mongrel but disciplined army, Aëtius pursued the Huns and defeated them at the famous battle of the Catalaunian Fields (it was actually fought near Troyes) at the end of August. Europe, the as yet unborn Europe, was saved on that day.

Aëtius did not follow up his victory: he was thinking of the balance of power, and had no desire to aggrandize the Visigoths, whom he had induced to fight as his allies against his old friend. Next year, therefore, Attila was still able to mount a campaign. He again approached Italy, and seized the hitherto inviolable fortress of Aquileia.[1] His European advisers, the Roman Orestes and the Greek Onegeses, advised him to move on Rome – of which Orestes' own son was to be the last emperor. Attila was just about to cross the Mincio,[2] when he was confronted by a solemn procession, chanting hymns and headed by no less a person than Pope Leo himself. No one knows what the two men said to each other. On his return all that Leo would say to Valentinian was: "Let us give thanks to God for he has delivered us from great danger." The incident had vast echoes: it shewed that, despite all the pagans might say, it was the Church which prevailed where they did not.[3]

Within the year Attila, who had retired on the promise of a tribute, was dead: marriage at the age of nearly seventy to a lusty young German girl had proved too much for the man

[1] It is traditionally on this occasion that refugees retired to Malamocco and Rialto, and so founded Venice; in fact, it was almost certainly at the time of the Lombard invasions in the following century.

[2] Milton's "smooth-sliding Mincius". It rises in Lake Garda and is a tributary of the Po.

[3] Legend has battened on the episode. It is the subject of Raphael's famous picture in the Vatican and of the finale of Act 1 of Verdi's *Attila*.

who had ravished half Europe. He was found in a fit on the
bridal bed.

With Attila, so rapid can be the changes of the kaleidoscope,
the Hun menace, too, was extinct.

Within a century the Vandals had spent themselves: ener-
vated by the delights of Carthage they fell at the first assault
of Belisarius and his 15,000 in 533. They are not heard of
again. And here is the paradox. When Rome and her empire
were dissolving, the two powers, Vandals and Huns, who act-
ively rejected and opposed her, left no trace: it was those who
while devouring her still loved and revered her who were to
endure, and whose children endure still.[1]

3. The rest of the sad story is soon told. Valentinian could
not forgive Aëtius for having saved Europe. He assassinated
him with his own hand, and shortly afterwards met the same
fate himself. In 455 Aëtius was succeeded as master of the
troops by Ricimer. Ricimer was of pure German descent, and
a capable soldier. Like Aëtius, he was called upon to confront
the Vandals, which he did with some success. His domestic
policy, however, was different from that of Aëtius. There was
now no legitimate representative of the Theodosian dynasty.
Ricimer therefore assumed the rôle not of prime minister but
of king-maker, relying on the support of yet another wave of
German newcomers.

Valentinian's successor, Maximus, was killed while trying to
escape from Rome during Gaiseric's invasion. He was succeeded by a Gallo-Roman, Avitus. He lasted only a year:
Ricimer had him deposed, and forcibly consecrated as bishop.
He died soon after. Ricimer was in no hurry to see another
emperor elected. Eventually, in 457, the emperor of the east,
Leo, made Ricimer *patricius*, and named Majorian, a soldier
of proven worth, as master of the troops. A few months later,
senate and army combined to make him emperor. Majorian
was a man of resolution and vigour. He at once set about
restoring order in Gaul, where the supporters of the deposed
Avitus and their Visigoth allies were making headway.
Majorian defeated them, moved on into Spain and there
assembled a fleet of 300 vessels to assault the Vandals; but this
expedition, like every other aimed at Gaiseric, was defeated by
his enterprise and subtlety. In 460 Majorian, too, fell the
victim of Ricimer's jealousy. With his death the end of the

---

[1] Corneille's *Attila* (1667) is concerned with the choice which Attila is
represented as having to make between decadent Rome and nascent France.

empire is brought a stage nearer. Both Visigoths and Vandals considered themselves absolved from the terms of the treaties they had made with him.

When Ricimer raised to the imperial throne a certain Severus, the provincial governors of Gaul and Dalmatia set themselves up as independent rulers. In 465 Severus died, and the west remained without an emperor for two years. Ricimer was content to rule alone. In 467 the emperor Leo, alarmed at Gaiseric's raids on the Peloponnese, sent to Rome as emperor Anthemius, a son-in-law of the emperor Marcian, together with his daughter, who was destined to be Ricimer's bride. The idea was that east and west, thus combined, should unite to crush Gaiseric. The great design was promoted at enormous expense. Inevitably, it ended in disaster. The Visigothic king, Euric, was thus encouraged to make himself ruler of all Gaul. Once again, Ricimer's patience was exhausted: in 472 he marched on Rome, and entered it in July. Another puppet, Olybrius, who was connected by blood with the Theodosian house, and by marriage with Gaiseric, was emperor for a few months. Ricimer, who for sixteen years had championed Rome after his fashion, died in August 472. Olybrius followed him in October. Only in March 473 did Ricimer's successor Gundobad proclaim Glycerius emperor, to be succeeded at the end of the year by Julius Nepos, a nominee of Constantinople.

It was Orestes, the secretary of Attila, who was to provide Nepos with a successor and Rome with its last emperor. In 475 he forced Nepos to flee first to Ravenna and then to his native Dalmatia. Orestes proclaimed as emperor his son, Romulus Augustulus.[1]

The barbarian mercenaries now demanded that they be allotted one-third of the soil of Italy as their free and unfettered domain. Orestes refused their demand. The Germans elected Odovacer as their king. He defeated Orestes and killed him. Romulus Augustulus became the captive of Odovacer, who, touched by the boy's beauty, dismissed him to live as a pensioner in Campania. Rome's empire was at an end.

[1] Zeno continued to recognize Nepos, until his death in 480.

PART TWO

CHAPTER VIII

LIMBO

The Roman empire in the west was dead, but Rome lived on. This is the most arresting fact of this arresting century. Barbarian Rome: the phrase sounds like a contradiction in terms. It is as easy as it is natural to regard the sixty years which separate the occupation of Rome by Odovacer from its "liberation" by Belisarius as a humiliating regression, an ignoble capitulation to Arian savagery, which ended in a glorious restoration to the imperial and catholic fold. Were this true, had there been a clean break, had "time had a stop" in the year 476, then there would be no excuse for prolonging this study beyond the end of the last chapter: there would be nothing Roman left to write about. But history is nearly always more subtle than historic events make it appear: epochs are prismatic, blending one from another to form the undivided and continuing light.

In fact, under Odovacer and his successor Theodoric, Rome was to enjoy a period of tranquillity such as she had not known since the days of the Antonines. Secondly, so spiritually powerful had Rome become that, despite the devastation of Belisarius' campaign[1] and the depredations of the Lombards for whose irruption it opened the way, Rome was able to transmit her ideas and her faith to posterity, so that they have passed like a laser through the thickest barriers of ignorance and opposition to illuminate our own days. It is to the examination of this double phenomenon, the vigour of un-Roman Rome, and the Roman spirit which it fostered, that the following chapters of this work will be directed.

The rise of Odovacer was briefly sketched at the conclusion of Part One. It must how be considered in more detail.[2]

[1] This lasted from 536 to 553. Lord Wavell used to hold that it was the setting of the most brilliant feat of arms of one of the world's greatest generals, as it undoubtedly was; but it ruined Italy, which was thus in no state to resist her next invaders, the Lombards.

[2] The original sources for the lives of Odovacer and Theodoric are plentiful but discursive: we have no continuous history or documentation. The chief ones are the following:

Odovacer was a Rugian; his father had been a general and minister of Attila, whom he represented as ambassador at the court of Constantinople, and whose life he saved there by disclosing a palace plot to murder him. Odovacer, although he was the son of so eminent a prince, began his military career as a spearman in the household troop. His ambition was kindled by a Pannonian monk called Severinus. The Anonymous[1] and the *Life* of the saint tell the story.

"When some barbarians [they were Goths] were on their way to Italy, they turned aside and went to call on Severinus, so as to obtain his blessing. Among them was Odovacer, who afterwards ruled over Italy, a young man miserably clad but of fine stature. When he bowed his head so as not to touch the roof of the very low cell, he learned from the man of God that he would win glory. When Odovacer bade him farewell Severinus said to him: 'Go on to Italy; go on, dressed in wretched skins: soon you will be able to give much to many.' Meanwhile, as the servant of God had foretold, Odovacer soon entered Italy and received the kingdom. At that same time king Odovacer recalled the prophecy which he had heard the holy man pronounce and at once wrote him a friendly letter in which he said he would grant anything the saint might think worth asking for. Severinus asked that a certain man who had been banished should be pardoned. Odovacer gratefully granted his request."[2]

As already related, it was by his defeat first of Orestes and then of Paulus that Odovacer became master of Italy. His treatment of Romulus Augustulus astonishes us by its generosity. True, the boy was young and handsome, but that would have availed him nothing at the hands of earlier Greeks or Romans. Was he not also the son of Orestes, Odovacer's defeated rival? Among the Hellenistic monarchs it had been "an axiom" that a king on succeeding to the throne killed off all his brothers. Augustus himself had not scrupled to murder

Ennodius, bishop of Pavia, was a contemporary of the two kings and pane-gyrist of Theodoric.

Cassiodorus (480–575). His *Varia* is a rich mine of information.

"*Anonymous Valesii*", an unknown author who wrote in barbarous Latin about 550, so called because first edited by Henri de Valois from one manu-script in 1636. Deals mainly with Theodoric.

Count Marcellinus, Justinian's chancellor.

Malchus, a page.

[1] 10, 46.
[2] The foregoing is quoted from the *Life*.

I THE CATAPHRACT

This unique piece, now in the National Museum at Damascus, comes from Doura-Europos, the Roman frontier post on the upper Euphrates. It is made of bronze scales (cf. Ammianus: see p. 35) fixed on a piece of cloth. Two rectangular sections are held together by a band of leather ending in a tail-guard and pierced in the middle, for the saddle. Size: 1·22 × 1·69 metres.

PLATE 1

PLATE 2

II ROMAN LIFE

The villa

Mosaic of a Roman villa, from Tabarka, North Africa, now in the Bardo Museum, Tunis. This mosaic has been chosen because it is more representative of the ordinary country-house of a fourth-century or fifth-century provincial Roman than more elaborate designs, some of which shew circular colonnades, with swags between the pillars, baths and other annexes. The very rich could certainly afford such luxuries (cf. p. 119 for such a villa in southern Gaul). The mosaic here reproduced shews an average "grange", with a barn and storerooms on the ground floor (note the high doorways to admit the entry of loaded wagons, just as in old English coaching-inns) with spacious and airy living-quarters above which have doors leading on to a raised patio. Thus early we have the prototype of the *piano nobile* of the Italian villa. The materials are stone (walls, domes and right-hand doorway), wood (left-hand and upper doorways) and tiles for gabled roofs. Olive-trees and poultry complete the tranquil domestic scene.

A. Mosaic of Ulysses and the Sirens, in the Bardo Museum, Tunis.

Interior decoration (see A to H)

Mosaics were extensively used for floor decoration. The stock themes were either mytho-logical subjects or local flora and fauna. The two Virgil mosaics are of great interest. Virgil held in the Roman mind a place of quite exceptional honour. In the region of Carthage he was specially venerated because he had devoted some of his most poignant verses to Dido, the Carthaginian queen. Even in remote Britain this theme was cele-brated.

B. Mosaic of Neptune, with a halo, in the Bardo Museum.

C. Virgil between the Tragic and Epic Muses, from Sousse, now in the Bardo Museum.
The scroll is open at *Aeneid* I, line 11:

Musa mihi causas memora, quo numine laeso

or, in Dryden's version:

O Muse! the causes and the crimes relate,
What goddess was provoked, and whence her hate.

PLATE 4

D. A Virgilian mosaic of about A.D. 350 from Low Ham, in Dorset, now in the Dorset Museum. The work is far cruder than that of the Sousse masterpiece. It shews, from left to right, Aeneas, his son Ascanius, Venus and Anna, Dido's sister.

PLATE 5

E. A mosaic, now in the Bardo Museum, shewing a horse and an elephant, the two animals for which Roman Africa was most noted.

PLATE 6

PLATE 7

F. A mosaic from El Djem, now in the Bardo Museum, shewing a hunting-scene. It is really just a battue of terrified animals.

G. Not only beasts, but men, too, fell victims to the Romans' passion for slaughter. This fourth-century mosaic in the Villa Borghese in Rome – it came from Torre Nuova – shews a typical group of gladiators, some naked, some armoured and all identified by name.

PLATE 8

H. For sheer vacuity it would be hard to beat the faces of the spectators in this representation of a fifth-century circus-scene from Gafsa, now in the Bardo Museum. It is the epitome of a society in spiritual decay.

PLATE 9

Theodosius I (379-395), from a gold *solidus* struck at Trier, now in the British Museum. The emperor is shewn wearing a diadem. The reverse shews Victory between the two seated emperors.

Arcadius, from a gold *solidus* struck at Constantinople, now in the British Museum. The emperor is shewn helmeted, holding spear and shield. The reverse shews Constantinople, holding a sceptre in one hand and Victory standing on a globe in the other.

Arcadius (395–408), from a statue in the National Archaeological Museum at Istanbul. The face shows the tension and anxiety of its epoch.

Valentinian I (364–375), from a statue in the National Archaeological Museum at Istanbul.

PLATE 11

Honorius, from a gold *solidus* struck at Milan, now in the British Museum. The emperor is shewn wearing a diadem and holding a sceptre. The reverse shews the emperor seated, holding a sceptre.

Romulus Augustulus (475–476), from a gold *solidus* struck at Milan, now in the British Museum. This pathetic coin shews the last of the Roman emperors helmeted, holding spear and shield. The reverse shews Victory, holding a cross.

Honorius (395–423), from a diptych from Aosta, in the cathedral.

IV ART AND ARCHITECTURE – SURVIVAL AND DECAY

Sarcophagus of Constantine

This magnificent work, now in the Pio-Clementine Vatican Museum, is worthy of its association. It is a grand example of an imperial tradition, classical, restrained and vigorous. It is a complete contrast to other contemporary work in the same material, porphyry – e.g. the group shewn on the opposite page.

PLATE 12

The Tetrachs, in Venice

For the best criticism of this strange composition, of the same epoch as the foregoing, see
p. 120.

PLATE 13

The Arch of Constantine: two details

This arch was dedicated in the year 315; and yet it shews every sign of falling off, of deficiency in inspiration and workmanship – see p. 120.

Cupola of Sta Costanza, Rome

By contrast with the foregoing, this church, built a generation later, has preserved the true classical style and line. Already innovations are appearing, notably the use of stone "cushions" between the capitals of the pillars and the springing of the arches, and the employment of mosaics in the vaults. These are not yet of glass: they are simply the ordinary floor-mosaics, with the ordinary subjects, such as birds and foliage, or *putti* at a vintage-festival, admirably executed, transferred from floor to ceiling. But this building may rightly be described as the last truly Roman building in Rome.

PLATE 15

PLATE 16

Half of the Nicomachi–Symmachi diptych

Now in the Victoria and Albert Museum: the other half is in the Musée de Cluny, Paris. Here, again, is an example of an art which is still in fine flower: this diptych is one of the most beautiful of late antique ivory carvings. It was executed at Rome in the late fourth century. It represents priestesses making sacrifice before an altar; and the diptych may have been commissioned to celebrate the profession of a priestess, a member of one of the two leading pagan families in Rome, themselves closely connected. It has also been suggested that the diptych was intended to commemorate a marriage between the same two families, either in 392–394 or in 401. The diptych was formerly in the Abbey of Moutier-en-Der, but disappeared probably when the monastery was suppressed in 1790. This leaf was bought for the Victoria and Albert Museum from a villager in 1865.

Stilicho

From the Monza diptych. Another example of this art, which possesses the additional interest that it may well be a genuine portrait of Stilicho (pp. 50-54).

PLATE 17

The Mildenhall dish

From remote Britain comes this final proof that the arts did not all decay suddenly and at once. Dated A.D. 300–460, this magnificent charger is probably of Gaulish workmanship. It came to light at Mildenhall in Suffolk, and is now in the British Museum.

V THEODORIC

This famous mosaic is part of a series which adorns the church of St Apollinare Nuovo at Ravenna. It shews Theodoric's palace, with a background of other public buildings. It employs the gold ground which begins to appear in wall mosaics in the fifth century, instead of the brown, turquoise or green of the preceding era. The design and structure are wholly in the classical tradition, and the very word PALATIUM proclaims Theodoric's determination to embody the continuity of the Roman Palatine. The curtains are not there merely for ornament and convenience: they are the mark of a royal residence. Their lineal descendants are the rich tapestries that adorn Christian basilicas on great feasts (cf. note 2 on p. 117). For the lay-out of the buildings of the palace see the article "A Byzantine Palace at Apollonia", by R. Goodchild in *Antiquity*, XXXIV, 1960.

The tomb of Theodoric

This monument stands on the outskirts of Ravenna. It is an eloquent mixture of the Roman and the barbaric. The cupola is supplied by one single block of stone, estimated to weigh 300,000 kilograms, or rather over 300 tons.

PLATE 19

PLATE 20

VI THE SAXON SHORE

Richborough

Rutupiae was the most important link in the chain of fortresses which defended the shores of Britain from Saxon raiders (see p. 42 and map on p. 41). From almost the earliest contacts of Rome with Britain, *Rutupiae* had been the chief port of entry. With Hadrian's Wall, it can claim to be one of the two most important Roman monuments to be seen in Britain today.

VII CHRISTIAN ART AND LIFE

Punic inscription

In the Bardo Museum. Child sacrifice had died out in Carthage some centuries before the age of Augustine; but its memory, and the cruelty which inspired it, survived in hundreds of inscriptions, in the Punic tongue, such as the one here illustrated. They were set up over the "tophets" in which the remains of the burned babies were deposited. In Africa, therefore, the Christian faith had to contend not only with imported Roman barbarism, but with the dark memories of national savagery.

PLATE 21

The Good Shepherd
Relief in the Bardo Museum. Early Christian art was in the nature of things derivative. A favourite theme was the Good Shepherd. This example shews an early stage in its development.

Relief from Carthage. Here a wholly new vigour is being applied to a traditional subject. In particular note the treatment of the hands.

PLATE 22

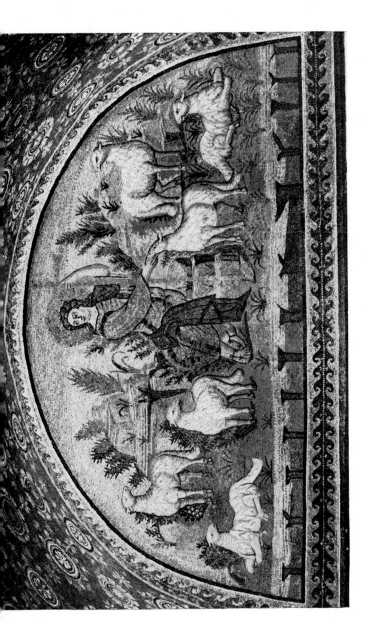

Mosaic at Ravenna

This mosaic, one of a series in the so-called Tomb of Galla Placidia is of great interest. It is instinct with *Romanitas*, and in its easy naturalness seems to recall the period of the early empire; but there is also in the detail, as in the material, a feeling of the Orient. The Good Shepherd is here well on the way to becoming the Christian Apollo.

PLATE 23

Font from Kelibia

Here all the art of the mosaicist is directed to the embellishment of a Christian font. It is of the cruciform pattern usual in the early cen-turies of the Christian era, the adult baptizand standing in the central depression and the priest in one of the arms.

PLATE 4

Baptism of Christ at Ravenna

This mosaic in the cupola of the Arian Baptistry at Ravenna is of the sixth century. It is of far more than merely decorative interest. It is a pictorial epitome of Arian theology. Christ is represented as secondary in stature and dignity to the Baptist and the symbolic figure of the River Jordan: only when the Holy Spirit, in the form of the Dove, conveys to Him the heavenly commission does He become wholly divine.

PLATE 25

Cross mosaic from Ibeitha

Now in the Bardo Museum. Here the Cross is used in a frankly decorative fashion, with flowers and the Alpha and Omega. The Faith has come a long way from the gloom of the catacombs.

PLATE 26

Christ in Glory, with Saints

This famous mosaic, in the apse of the church of Sta Pudenziana in Rome, is notable not only for the dignity, still classical, of the figures, but because it is the oldest surviving representation of the church of the Holy Sepulchre in Jerusalem. It shews the basilica erected by Constantine, the shrine over the Sepulchre itself and the cross on Calvary still unenclosed. It was only in the days of the Crusaders that all three sites were brought under the one roof we see to-day. The mosaic is late fourth century, partly restored.

PLATE 27

Pavement from Hinton St Mary

As shewn by Professor Jocelyn Toynbee, this detail from a mosaic of the fourth century, brought to light in 1963 at Hinton St Mary in Dorset, is the earliest known representation of Christ to be found in Britain. (See *Journal of Roman Studies*, LIV, December 1964, pp. 7–14.)

PLATE 28

Hippo Regius

The great basilica, or basilica of Peace, Augustine's metropolitan church. It had three aisles, and the floor was covered with elaborate mosaics, portions of which may still be seen. The episcopal throne is visible behind the high altar, at the end of the central apse, the usual place for the bishop's seat in early churches. In England Norwich cathedral has preserved this ancient custom.

The Forum, built in A.D. 77-8, is the largest in Africa, 81 metres by 54 metres overall – in exact accord with the proportions recommended by Vitruvius (V, i, 2). The floor and columns of the peristyle are of marble. (See article by E. Marec in *Libya*, 1954, Tome 11, pp. 363 *seq.*)

PLATE 29

St Ambrose
The mosaic portrait in
Milan: see p. 133.

PLATE 30

St Jerome

We have no contemporary portrait of St Jerome; but such was his hold on later centuries, specially of the Renaissance, that few saints were more often represented by their painters – his popularity far exceeded that of either St Ambrose or St Augustine. This portrait by El Greco, the Cretan Domenikos Theotokopoulos (1541–1614), is of special interest as shewing how the great western doctor appealed to the great eastern painter. It is in the Frick Collection, New York.

PLATE 31

The Cross of Lothair

This famous jewel may be said to represent the romantic epilogue of the imperial drama. It shews a cameo of Augustus, the founder of the empire, set in a cross, the symbol of the new Rome which succeeded his. The rock-crystal seal set near the foot of the cross is that of Lothair II of Lotheringia (855–869), the son of the emperor Lothair I. The cross is in the treasury at Aachen, the capital of his great-grandfather Charlemagne.

PLATE 32

his own kin, Cleopatra's son by his great-uncle Julius. Nor
had later emperors shewn mercy to the progeny of a defeated
opponent. Yet here was the barbarian *arriviste* doing that very
thing, and granting the lad a splendid and historic villa near
Cape Misenum, built by Marius and decorated by Lucullus
five and a half centuries before, together with an annual
pension of 6,000 *solidi*.[1] A new and gentler spirit seems to have
entered the Roman world with these Arian outsiders, although,
as Odovacer was to learn, it would not always prevail.

In succession to three of the "shadow emperors" who still
survived,[2] Odovacer was now undisputed master of Italy.
What would be his relations with Byzantium? Would he seek
the purple for himself, or would he declare himself to be an
independent monarch, like Gaiseric before him? Odovacer
did neither: he decided to compromise, thus introducing into
western politics yet another unknown, and northern, quality.

After his state entry into Rome and tacit recognition by the
senate, Odovacer sought formal recognition of his authority
from Constantinople. With disarming tact he consigned to
the emperor Zeno the imperial insignia, his embassy (sent
ostensibly by Romulus, as though to underline Odovacer's
modesty) being instructed to ask in return simply that Odovacer
be granted the title Patrician. Italy, they were to say, had no
need of a separate ruler: the empire was one and indivisible.
Zeno, who had himself but recently undergone the vicissitudes
of deposition and restoration, was only too happy to be given
so graceful an opportunity of recognizing the *fait accompli*.
Odovacer was to rule for thirteen years (476–489). Whether
he or his successor ever styled themselves "kings of Italy" is not
clear; but as Hodgkin puts it:[3] "Odovacer and Theodoric
were, without all contradiction, kings; if not 'kings of Italy', at
any rate 'kings in Italy', sometimes actually making war on
the Caesar of Byzantium, and not caring, when they did so,
to set up the phantom of a rival Emperor in order to legitimise
their opposition." It must be remembered that in Roman
ears the title king did not carry any such exalted connotation
as it does in ours. To a Roman a king was a "client", an "ally",

---

[1] The site is now occupied by the Castel dell' Ovo.

[2] The phrase is that of Thomas Hodgkin, whose *Theodoric the Goth: the Barbarian Champion of Civilisation* is the classic book on the subject. The quotation comes from p. 104. The survivors were Glycerius, Nepos and Romulus.

[3] *op. cit.*, p. 104.

H

who obeyed Rome's bidding until such time as Rome was ready to absorb his realms into its own dominion. Such had been the fate of the kings of Cappadocia, of Numidia, of Judaea (the Herods, the most famous of all), of Arabia. As Tacitus put it, "Rome made even kings the instruments of servitude." Thus the use of the title "king" would not in itself assert autonomy. But Odovacer's behaviour clearly shews that, far from seeking to establish his independence, he regarded himself as the vicegerent of the emperor. When in 480 Nepos was assassinated, Odovacer, as though he were the avenger commissioned by Zeno, led a punitive expedition against the murderers, defeated and killed their leader and restored Dalmatia to the Italian jurisdiction. He refused to aid one Illus who revolted against the emperor. He had already, as the emperor's deputy, ceded Narbonne to the Visigoths, and it was Odovacer who had concluded with Gaiseric the treaty of 477,[1] whereby Sicily was retroceded to Italy, subject to the payment of tribute and the retention by Gaiseric of a castle which he had built in the island, just as modern powers retain "military bases" in territories which they restore to their rightful inhabitants.

Such is our scanty, if significant, knowledge of Odovacer's external achievements. With his internal policy we are better acquainted. It was said at the end of the last chapter that the barbarian mercenaries had demanded "a third" of the land of Italy. Hodgkin,[2] while not denying this, suggests that the distribution was never completely carried out. Professor Dumoulin, writing some twenty years later,[3] argues that "such a proceeding would certainly have led to some disturbance, of which we can find no evidence in any part of the country". Hodgkin makes this same point. Besides, says Dumoulin, neither Odovacer's followers nor those of Theodoric were plentiful enough to occupy a third part of the total area of Italy. What appears to have been allotted to them was a third of the *ager publicus*, or state domains. On these, owing to the progressive depopulation of the countryside, there would be ample accommodation for new occupiers. The newcomers restored prosperity to Italy; for now that the traditional external sources of the supply of grain were in alien hands, the Italian harvest became once again a prime factor in the

[1] See p. 81 above.
[2] *op. cit.*, p. 105.
[3] *Cambridge Medieval History*, Vol. I, p. 446.

life of the country; so much so that, stimulated by this necessity, Italy, which had for centuries imported corn as a tribute, was soon able to export it at a profit.

Odovacer deliberately maintained, even enhanced, the established authorities of Rome. The senate he regarded as his partner; it was in their joint names that statues were raised to Zeno in the western capital. In 477 the record of consuls had been interrupted: in 482 it was resumed. The administration continued to work: Pelagius became praetorian prefect, and proved himself as traditionally rapacious as any of his predecessors. Most significant of all, Odovacer, an Arian, shewed every deference to the Pope. Simplicius, who adorned the throne of St Peter from 468 to 483, recognized the king's authority. On his death a conference of the senate and clergy jointly resolved that no new election should take place before consultation with the representative of "the king", as he is styled in the report of the proceedings.[1]

It was the small-minded jealousy of his titular overlord that undid this tolerant and efficient northerner. As related above, after defeating Nepos, in 480 Odovacer had annexed Dalmatia to the Italian "diocese". Whether Dalmatia came within the eastern or the western region of the theoretically undivided empire had for long been a vexed and vexing question.[2] By his action Odovacer had presumed to answer it, and thus brought his authority uncomfortably near to Constantinople. Zeno's suspicion was rekindled four years later by Odovacer's correspondence with Illus. As we have seen, Odovacer refused his help to the would-be usurper; but two years later Zeno persuaded himself that the king was disposed to reverse his loyal policy. Zeno therefore deliberately fomented a quarrel between Odovacer and Feletheus, king of the Rugians, the powerful ruler of the Danubian lands from which Odovacer had migrated into Italy. This, thought the emperor, would keep Odovacer busy and dissipate any possible threat to his own pre-eminence. Unfortunately, Odovacer's victory over Feletheus was as crushing as it was swift. What expedient now remained to be exploited by the craven and crafty Zeno? It is at this juncture that Theodoric enters the story, nor should our distaste for the dishonourable intrigues which advanced him, our sympathy for Odovacer, and particularly his terrible

[1] *Cambridge Medieval History*, Vol. I, p. 436.

[2] Even to-day the traveller in Jugoslavia is struck by this east–west ambivalence.

end at the hand of his rival, cause us to underestimate Theodoric's claim to be included among the "Heroes of the Nations".

"Theodoric the Ostrogoth," writes Hodgkin in the *Introduction* of his biography, "is one of those men who did great deeds and filled a large space in the eyes of their contemporaries, but who, not through their own fault, but from the fact that the stage of the world was not yet ready for their appearance, have failed to occupy the very first rank among the founders of empires and the moulders of the fortunes of the human race.

"He was born into the world at the time when the Roman empire in the West was staggering blindly to ruin, under the crushing blows inflicted upon it by two generations of barbarian conquerors. That Empire had been for more than six centuries indisputably the strongest power in Europe, and had gathered into its bosom all that was best in the civilization of the nations that were settled round the Mediterranean Sea. Rome had given her laws to all these peoples, had, at any rate in the West, made their roads, fostered the growth of their cities, taught them her language, administered justice, kept back the barbarians of the frontier, and for great spaces of time preserved 'the Roman peace' throughout their habitations. Doubtless there was another side to this picture: heavy taxation, corrupt judges, national aspirations repressed, free peasants sinking down into hopeless bondage. Still it cannot be denied that during a considerable part of its existence the Roman empire brought, at least to the western half of Europe, material prosperity and enjoyment of life which it had not known before, and which it often looked back to with vain regrets when the great empire had fallen into ruins. But now, in the middle of the fifth century, when Theodoric was born amid the rude splendour of an Ostrogothic palace, the unquestioned ascendancy of Rome over the nations of Europe was a thing of the past. There were still two men, one at the Old Rome by the Tiber, and the other at the New Rome by the Bosphorus, who called themselves August, Pious and Happy,[1] who wore the diadem and the purple shoes of Diocletian, and professed to be the joint lords of the universe. Before the Eastern Augustus and his successors there did in truth lie a long future of dominion, and once or twice they were to recover no inconsiderable

---

[1] In the year 218 Elagabalus, in writing to the senate, had called himself *Pius Felix Invictus Augustus*, which henceforth became the official style of the emperors.

portion of the broad lands which had formerly been the heritage
of the Roman people. But the Roman empire at Rome was
stricken with an incurable malady. The three sieges and the
final sack of Rome by Alaric (410) revealed to the world that
she was no longer 'Roma Invicta', and from that time forward
every chief of Teutonic or Slavonic barbarians who wandered
with his tribe over the wasted plains between the Danube
and the Adriatic might cherish the secret hope that he, too,
would one day be drawn in triumph up the Capitolian Hill,
through the crowded ranks of the slavish citizens of Rome, and
that he might be lodged on the Palatine in one of the sumptuous
palaces which had been built long ago for 'the lords of the
world'."

Such was the era into which Theodoric was born, such the
hope that he cherished. Theodoric was an Amal by birth, son
of Theodemir, king of the Goths, and of Erelieva his wife.
He entered the world under the best possible auspices, for on
that very day in the year 454 (or perhaps 452 – we cannot be
sure) there arrived a messenger from Theodemir's brother,
Walamir, that he had routed a Hunnish army, and had sent
the remnant of it in headlong flight to the deserts of Scythia.
So the boy was called Thiuda-reiks, or *people-ruler*, a name which
Latin historians, perhaps on the analogy of Theodosius,
changed to Theodoricus.[1] Not long after Theodoric's birth,
the Ostrogoths became involved in a war with the emperor
of the east. They were settled in Pannonia, and, in accordance
with the established pattern, were regarded as *federates*. As
such, they were entitled to pay "and this pay, which was called
wages when the empire was strong, and tribute when it was
weak, consisted, partly at any rate, of heavy chests of imperial
aurei, sent as *strenae* or New Year Presents, to the barbarian
king and his chief nobles".[2] About the year 461 the emperor
Leo for some reason withheld the *strenae* – perhaps he had
none to send. The Ostrogoths sent an embassy to Constantinople to complain. They returned with the news that not only
were the *strenae* to be withheld indefinitely, but that to make
matters far worse, they were to be paid to another Goth, a

---

[1] Greek historians generally call him Theoderichos. Jordanes uses both
spellings. Since we cannot now get back to the original Thiuda-reiks, it
seems best to give him the name by which he is best known.

[2] Hodgkin, *op. cit.*, p. 36. He notes that the *solidus aureus*, the chief imperial coin of this time, was worth about twelve shillings [pre-1914]; and
that *strenae* is the same word as the French *étrennes*.

low-born pretender also called, confusingly enough, Theodoric, but with the addition Strabo, "Squinter". The Squinter was a brother-in-law, or nephew, of a jumped-up barbarian called Aspar, who had already placed two emperors on the throne, and the Squinter no doubt owed his elevation to his relative's influence.

The reply of the legitimate Ostrogoths to this double insult was rapid and radical: they simply laid waste nearly the whole of the province of Illyricum. The emperor at once changed his mind, despatched the arrears of *strenae* and again sought the friendship of the Goths, promising that all future stipends would be paid on the nail. He only asked that, as a guarantee of the peace, Theodemir's son should be sent to Constantinople as a hostage. Thus it came about that little Theodoric, then rising eight, entered the charmed circle of the imperial court. His handsome face and his good manners soon made him a favourite of the emperor.

Theodoric, like Ataulf before him,[1] soon realized the virtues of *civilitas*, of the ordered life of a stable state. He was quick also to appreciate the weakness of the Byzantine régime, with its endless intrigues, its hypocrisies, treacheries and deceptions. He was no scholar, and according to the Anonymous[2] for the first ten years of his reign never learned to write even the four letters necessary for endorsing his edicts, and therefore had a golden stencil made for LEGI (I have read) or perhaps THEOD, which he used to trace his signature. Hodgkin says he has "a slight mistrust of this story, because it is told in almost the same words [by Procopius, *Anecdota*, 6,15] of the contemporary Justin I, Emperor of the East". It may well be true, though: it would be quite possible for a popular and athletic youth to reach the age of eighteen without having found the time to master a foreign script – it would be enough for his purposes to be able to speak it fluently and persuasively.

A Gold Multiple of Theodoric, preserved in the *Museo Nazionale* at Rome, shews his head and shoulders. He is dressed in what looks like gold armour of Roman pattern. Behind his left shoulder is the figure of winged victory standing on an orb which was the traditional talisman of the emperors. The face is that of a spirited northerner, with a long nose, prominent eyes and a firm mouth surmounted by a neat little moustache. The most distinctively "nordic" feature is his hair, which descends in a "waterfall" cut, with tassel-like curls at the

---

[1] p. 71 above.   [2] Section 79: Hodgkin, p. 145.

ends, suggestive of the renaissance dandy. The inscription is *Rex Theodericus Pius Princis.*

When Theodoric was nineteen, the emperor Leo sent him home to his father, together with costly gifts. Walamir having been killed in action against the Scyri, beyond the Danube, Theodemir was now chief king of the Ostrogoths. Young Theodoric decided to prove himself a worthy heir. In order to demonstrate immediately and decisively that ten years as an imperial favourite had not softened his native fibre, he collected a little band of 6,000 men from among his admirers and dependents, crossed the Danube and proceeded to chastise a certain Babai, who had been boasting of his victory over a Roman army. Theodoric killed Babai, took his family prisoner and occupied the key frontier post of Singidunum (Belgrade).

With such a son to second him, Theodemir now felt powerful enough to seek new conquests. But where? There could be but one goal, the eastern empire. The ensuing raid was not a success, and as a result of the negotiations which terminated it Theodemir was left with but six towns in the north-east corner of the Aegean, including Pella, the birth-place of Alexander the Great. But when in or about 474 Theodemir died, Theodoric succeeded to the kingship by general acclaim. In 474, too, the emperor Leo died, and was succeeded by an Isaurian chieftain called Tarasicodissa, more easily and generally known as Zeno. He owed his elevation to a palace plot; and by a palace plot in November of the following year he was forced to flee to his native Isauria. Yet two years later, in July 477, Zeno was back again. During these dubious manoeuvres the Squinter had backed the usurper, Basilicus, whereas Theodoric had remained loyal to Zeno. The grateful Isaurian now rewarded the twenty-four-year-old Goth by making him a Patrician and Master of the Soldiery and proclaimed him his adopted son, high honours indeed for so youthful a "barbarian". With the Squinter's death in 481, Theodoric became one of the most powerful men in the empire. Zeno made him Consul in 484, and it was when holding this august office that he defeated the rebel Illus. He was granted a triumph two years later, and his equestrian statue was placed in one of the squares of Byzantium.

The shifty Isaurian, in reality more barbaric than his barbarian protégé, now felt for Theodoric the same ambivalent esteem as he did for Odovacer: he had needed and relied on both, he would be happier without either. To divide, he thought, would be to rule.[1] Odovacer had, perhaps, been in collusion with Illus, Theodoric had beyond question defeated him: let him now supplant Odovacer; that would be only just – and how convenient, too.

By so shabby a contrivance was Theodoric launched against Odovacer. In 488 he entered Odovacer's territory with his Goths. The campaign lasted five years. From the Isonzo Odovacer retreated to Verona; beaten there, to Ravenna. After inconclusive exchanges, in August 490 Theodoric encamped in the same pine forest which Odovacer had occupied when opposed to Orestes. The siege was to last three years, during which Theodoric subdued almost the whole of Italy. Although Theodoric was, like Odovacer, an Arian, he seems from the first to have enjoyed the powerful patronage of the Church. The bishop of Milan had opened the gates of that city to him, the bishop of Pavia did likewise; and Theodoric tactfully entrusted his mother and sister to the protection of the accommodating prelate. Finally, it was the bishop of Ravenna who induced Odovacer to come to terms with his rival. The principal clause of the treaty assured to Odovacer not only his life but equality of power with his conqueror; "but of course," says Hodgkin,[2] "there was not, there could not be, any real peace on such terms between the two queen-bees in that swarming hive of barbarians". In the event, Theodoric, breaking his solemn undertaking, killed Odovacer with his own hand at a banquet, and the rest of his family were done to death soon afterwards.

It might be supposed that a reign inaugurated by such a shocking act of treachery would be marked by harshness, oppression and villainy. In fact, it was not: on the contrary, for the next thirty years Theodoric ruled with clemency, justice and devotion to the welfare of his subjects. Only at the end of his days did he shew once more the baser side of his character.

Our chief sources for Theodoric's rule are Roman and Orthodox; they are neither contemporary nor written by his countrymen. They condemn him for his persecution of the Catholics in his last two years. "Still, over the grave of this dead barbarian and heretic, when they have nothing to gain by speaking well of him, they cannot forbear to praise the noble impartiality

---

[1] This famous phrase had not yet been coined. *Divide ut imperes*, usually attributed to "the Romans" cannot in fact be traced farther back than the days of Louis XI (1423–83).

[2] *op. cit.*, p. 124.

and anxious care for the welfare of his people, which, for the
space of one whole generation, gave happiness to Italy."[1]

"He was an illustrious man," says the Anonymous,[2] "and
full of goodwill towards all. He reigned thirty-three [actually
thirty-two] years, and during thirty of these years so great was
the happiness of Italy that even the wayfarers were at peace.
For he did nothing wrong. He so governed the two races at
the same time, Romans and Goths, that although he himself
was of the Arian sect, he nevertheless made no assault on the
Catholic religion. He gave games in the circus and the amphitheatre, so that even by the Romans he was called a Trajan
or a Valentinian, whose times he took as his model. At the
same time the Goths rendered true obedience to their valiant
king, according to the Edict by which he established their
rights. Military service he kept on the same footing as under
the emperors. He was generous with gifts and the distribution
of grain, and although he found the treasury empty,[3] by his
efforts he recouped and enriched it.

"He gave one of his daughters in marriage to the King of
the Visigoths in Gaul, another to the son of the Burgundian
King; his sister to the King of the Vandals, and his niece to
the King of the Thuringians.[4] Thus he pleased all the nations
round him, for he was a great lover of manufactures and a
great restorer of cities. He repaired the aqueduct of Ravenna,
which Trajan had built; and again, after a long interval,
brought water into the city. He completed, but did not
dedicate, the palace, and finished the porticoes round it. At
Verona he erected baths and a palace, and constructed a
portico from the gate to the palace. The aqueduct, which
had long been destroyed, he renewed, and brought in water
through it. He also surrounded the city with new walls. At
Ticinum [Pavia] too he built a palace, baths and an amphitheatre, and erected walls round the city. On many other
cities also he bestowed similar gifts. Thus he so charmed the
nations near him that they entered into a league with him,
hoping that he would be their king. The merchants, too, from
divers provinces, flocked to his dominions, for so great was the

---

[1] Hodgkin, *op. cit.*, p. 128.

[2] Sections 59 *seq.*

[3] Literally "hay" – an interesting anticipation of the modern American-
ism.

[4] Theodoric himself married a sister of Clovis, king of the Franks, whose
baptism in 500 opened a new era for what was to become France.

order which he maintained that if anyone wanted to leave gold or silver on his land it was as safe as in a walled city. A proof of this was the fact that he never made gates for any city of Italy, and the gates already existing were never closed. Anyone who had business to transact could do it as safely by night as by day."

This picture in its civic achievement seems to go back to the days of Hadrian, in its dynastic tapestry forward to the Habsburgs. Its almost apocalyptic felicity might seem over-drawn; yet it is supported by Procopius, who could be as waspish and denigrating as any when he wanted to. He was no supporter of the king, far from it, and yet he writes:[1]

"Theodoric was an extraordinary lover of justice, and adhered rigorously to the laws. He guarded the country from barbarian invasions, and displayed the greatest intelligence and prudence. There was in his government scarcely a trace of injustice towards his subjects, nor would he permit any of those under him to attempt anything of the kind, except that the Goths divided among themselves the same proportion of the land of Italy which Odovacer had allotted to his partisans. Thus then Theodoric was in name a 'tyrant', but in truth a true king, not inferior to the best of his predecessors, and his popularity grew greatly, both among Goths and Italians, and this fact was contrary to the ordinary fashion of human affairs; for generally, as different classes of the state want different things, the government which pleases one party has to incur the enmity of those who do not belong to it."

In ecclesiastical affairs, Theodoric shewed the tolerance of his predecessor. He was an Arian, but he was always ready to support and cherish the Catholics: as related above, it was his policy to conciliate the bishops of northern Italy. Nor did he attempt to influence papal elections, so long as they were conducted peaceably; when, as happened in 498, there was a disputed election Theodoric intervened, but only as an arbitrator. He simply ordered that the candidate who had obtained the majority of the votes should be declared bishop of Rome. This condition was fulfilled by Symmachus, who was accordingly recognized as pope, his opponent, Laurentius being given a secondary see as a consolation prize. When, two years later, Theodoric visited Rome he was enthusiastically received by pope, senate and people, and set about a magnificent programme of restoration and adornment. But the

[1] *Gothic Wars*, V, i. 27.

dispute still smouldered, and was likely to be inflamed into
a schism,[1] because Laurentius was known to be in favour of
subservience to Byzantium, to which, in ecclesiastical matters,
recent popes had insisted that they could not subscribe. The
enemies of Symmachus rigged against him charges of mounting
gravity, first adultery, then peculation, finally the celebration
of Easter on the wrong day. It took no less than five synods to
settle the matter. When the contending parties applied to
Theodoric for a decision he pointed out that it was for them,
not for him, to accept the onus (and odium) of making the
award. "We order you to decide this matter which is of God,
and which we have confided to your care, as seems good to
you. Do not expect any judgement from us, for it is your duty
to settle the question." When the verdict was still withheld,
he writes once more: "I order you to obey the command of
God." At last they obeyed, and Symmachus was elected.

That Theodoric was a tolerant man, that he shewed an
impartiality in religious matters remarkable in a man of his
epoch, is beyond dispute – indeed, one example of his fairness
to be related shortly helped to alienate him from his subjects;
but it is only relevant to remember that Theodoric was no
theologian, that he was a northern layman, not a subtle Greek,
and that the distinctions which to the eastern mind seemed so
vital would appear to him as mere trichotomy. The deference
therefore which he paid to the Church, his insistence that it
must order its own affairs, is deeply significant of the stature
and influence which the Church had now won in the Roman
polity.

The foregoing résumé – for it is no more – of Theodoric's
policy and achievements will have shewn him, it is hoped, as
a wise, beneficent ruler, a man who increased the prosperity
of both Goths and Romans at home and their prestige and glory
abroad. When necessary, he had not hesitated to back his
diplomacy by force of arms, so that in addition to being one
of Rome's best rulers, and the architect of a united Italy such
as would not exist again for thirteen and a half centuries, he
was also regarded as the general protector of the Teutons,
and was to live in legend as such.[2] Above all, he had proved

[1] It is in fact known to Catholic historians as "the Laurentian schism",
or "the First Greek Schism". It was ended only by the death of Symmachus
in 514.

[2] In the *Nibelungenlied*, for instance, he is commemorated as Dietrich of
Bern [Theodoric of Verona].

that he, the northern newcomer, could rule as a Roman. It was the Roman spirit, the Roman fabric which he had cherished, enriched and transmitted. His palace at Ravenna was built in pure Roman style.[1]

It would be pleasant indeed to end the story of Theodoric here, to narrate the tranquil sunset which closed so glorious a day. Alas! that is not possible: the latter end of Theodoric was deplorable, and was the prelude to all the woe and degradation Italy was so soon, and for so long, to suffer.

A number of causes conspired to alienate the king from his subjects, to goad him to evil and to sully his fame.

Theodoric had always extended his tolerance very notably to the Jews. "We cannot impose a religion by force, since no one can be compelled to believe against his will," he said,[2] a remark which must have appeared to many in that age as almost heretical. In the year 523 the Jews of Ravenna fell under the suspicion of having ridiculed the Christian rite of baptism, apparently as a protest against attempted mass conversion, whereupon the Christian mob flung them into the river and burnt their synagogues. When the Jews complained to the king at Verona he ordered the Christians to rebuild the synagogues at their own expense. Disorders followed, whereupon the king forbade the citizens to carry arms, not even penknives being permitted.

Theodoric's Catholic subjects naturally resented this stern justice. Meanwhile, Theodoric's suspicions had been aroused by the accession of the emperor Justin, in 518, because Justin was as orthodox as he was illiterate, and it was clear that his accession would bode no good for the Arians. It is from this period that the mental and material deterioration of Theodoric must be dated. He suspected that the senators were playing a double game, and intriguing with Constantinople behind

[1] The Anonymous, Section 61, cites a telling aphorism of Theodoric: "A poor Roman plays the Goth, a rich Goth the Roman." The Romans were still, even by the Goths, accounted "top nation".

[2] Cassiodorus, *Var.* ii, 27: "*religionem imperare non possumus, quia nemo cogitur ut credat invitus.*" See *Letters of Cassiodorus*, ed. Hodgkin, 1886. Compared with the Catholics the Arians were naturally more inclined to be sympathetic with the Jews, if only because the Arians did not accept Christ as being wholly divine. The founder of the Arian sect was an elder of Alexandria who lived in the fourth century. He held that the Son was created by the Father, and subordinate to the Father, although of a similar nature with Him. This doctrine was condemned by the Council of Nicaea in 325, but Arianism was a living faith for many generations. The Christology of Islam is related to Arianism.

his back. Two senators seemed marked out to lead an "im-
perialist" party, if such could be formed, a nobleman of the
great Anician house called Symmachus and his son-in-law
Boethius, the Leonardo da Vinci of his day. At the king's
request he had constructed a sundial and water-clock for the
king of the Burgundians; he had translated Aristotle into
Latin: his treatise on Music was a classic. He had been Consul
in 510; twelve years later, his two sons, though mere lads,
had held the same august office. Until the year 523 no one
had stood higher in the royal favour than Boethius. Yet now
Boethius was arrested and flung into prison, because he had
dared to protest against the unjust accusation of treason brought
against an illustrious fellow-senator, Albinus, by an informer
called Cyprian. After the travesty of a trial, Boethius was condemned to death; "and the judges whose trembling lips pronounced the monstrous sentence were the very senators whose
cause he had tried to serve".[1] During the period which elapsed
between his imprisonment (he was confined at Pavia) and his
death he wrote the work by which he is universally known, the
Consolation of Philosophy. It was later to be translated into English
by King Alfred and by Geoffrey Chaucer, imitated by Sir
Thomas More, and rendered into every European tongue.
One authority says he was beheaded, another that he was
tortured, a cord being twisted round his forehead until his eyes
started from their sockets, the *coup de grâce* being dealt by a club.
Symmachus was put to death the following year, 525.

That very autumn[2] there arrived from Constantinople an
edict of the emperor Justin which inflamed the already-ailing
mind of Theodoric. The sovereign bigot had issued a decree
that all Arian churches in Constantinople should be closed, and
all Arians excluded from civil and military employment. This
harsh ordinance was now to be applied to Italy. It was a dusty
recompense to the man who for thirty years had shewn a
perfect tolerance to the Catholic Church, and in the disputed
papal election had actually suported the orthodox candidate.
Theodoric was bound to resent the edict and to attempt to
counter it. In doing so, he made the greatest diplomatic
blunder of his whole career: he ordered the pope, John I, to

---

[1] Hodgkin, *op. cit.*, p. 275.

[2] Dumoulin, in *Cambridge Medieval History*, Vol. I, p. 453, implies that the
condemnation of Boethius and Symmachus *followed* the issue of the edict;
but Bréhier has shewn that it preceded it (*Histoire de l'Église*, Vol. IV,
p. 435).

proceed to Constantinople and to exact from the emperor the cancellation of his decree.

The pope set out accompanied by a brilliant train of prelates, senators and noblemen. Not since the very earliest days of New Rome had a pope visited Constantinople; and the advent of the successor of St Peter at this juncture, so soon after the Laurentian schism, was the very act most likely to forge the union between pope and emperor which constituted Theodoric's greatest danger. And so it proved. The whole city turned out to greet them at the fifteenth milestone. The pope celebrated Christmas in Constantinople, and the emperor himself, although he had been crowned by the patriarch on his accession six years before, now received the diadem a second time from the hands of his apostolic guest. On the following Easter Day, 19th April, 526, he celebrated mass in St Sophia in Latin, and was awarded precedence over the patriarch.

The result of the mission fell far short of Theodoric's hopes. The emperor did, it is true, promise to restore their churches to the Arians, but refused to allow any Arian who had been converted to orthodoxy to revert to his former creed.

Theodoric, maddened by the realization of his own folly as much as by the obduracy of the emperor, seized the pope on his arrival at Ravenna and imprisoned him with his brother prelates. The pope died soon after. He was regarded as a martyr, and his corpse was transported to Rome and buried in St Peter's. In order to force the emperor's hand, Theodoric, on 26th August, issued, by the hand of a Jewish Treasury clerk, an edict which authorized the Arians to seize all Catholic churches. The edict was to come into force on the 30th. But that very day Theodoric, whose mind was now so unhinged that he imagined he saw the features of Symmachus in the head of a great fish that had been brought to his dinner-table, breathed his last, his end having been hastened by a violent attack of malaria.

So ended the great experiment. Theodoric's eclipse was miserable. The unity he had won was dissipated. Roman was arrayed against Goth, Arian against Catholic, Italy against Constantinople. Constantinople was to wreak a disastrous vengeance on the recalcitrant province. The Lombards, entering the peninsula as the allies of the emperor Justinian in 535, would return thirty years later as savage and rapacious conquerors. Rome itself would be besieged, occupied, sacked and left desolate. "The Lombard King and the Byzantine

Emperor," says Hodgkin in a noble epilogue,[1] "tore Italy in
pieces. Then the Frank descended from the Alps to join in
the fray. The German, the Saracen, the Norman made their
appearance on the scene. Not all wished to ravage and despoil;
some had high and noble purposes in their hearts, but, in fact,
they all tended to divide her. The Popes even at their best,
even while warring as Italian patriots against the foreign
Emperor, still divided their country. Last of all came the
Spaniard and the Austrian, by whom, down to our own day,[2]
Italy was looked upon as an estate, out of which kingdoms and
duchies might be carved at pleasure as appanages for younger
sons and compensations for lost provinces. Only at length,
towards the close of the nineteenth century, has Italy regained
that priceless boon of national unity, which might have been
hers before it was attained by any other country in Europe,
if only the ambition of emperors and the false sentiment of
'Roman' patriots would have spared the goodly tree which had
been planted in Italian soil by Theodoric the Ostrogoth."

And yet in other lands, and in other ages right down to our
own, offshoots of that very tree were to be transplanted and
to flourish. They flourish still. What was the nature of that
magic and indestructible seed? To an attempt to analyse its
essence the remaining chapters of this study will be devoted.

[1] *op. cit.*, p. 369.   [2] Written in 1890.

CHAPTER IX

THE THINGS WHICH ARE CAESAR'S

As suggested at the very outset of this survey, the decline of Rome has not seldom been attributed to the rise of the Christian faith. The two phenomena were contemporary, they were related; but it was not the new faith that enfeebled the old fabric. On the contrary, it was the growing consciousness of the inadequacy, the decay of the traditional sanctions and loyalties of the Roman world that led more and more souls to seek to pass through things temporal so that finally they should not lose the things which are eternal.

This fallacy, that Christianity caused the downfall of Rome, is as old as the downfall itself. Augustine, as we shall see,[1] devoted a large part of the *Civitas Dei* to a warm and witty refutation of it. But the very success of Augustine has led, through the ages, to what may be called a counter-fallacy, namely that as more and more spirits sought sanctuary in the new, the old not only decayed but disappeared altogether. This assumption is equally false. Religion is the backbone of history; but it supports many a secular limb. It is only by grasping this cardinal fact that we are able to understand the complicated pattern of fifth-century Roman society. That the state was moribund there is no doubt: the death of the old Rome was inevitable, for the reasons already outlined in the earlier chapters of this book, Christianity or no Christianity; it was nevertheless able, as so many organisms are, to transmit a life which it could no longer live.

Outwardly and officially, the empire was Christian, and the empire was one; as related in the last chapter, the new rulers of the west had no desire to erect alien polities on the ruins of native Rome, but rather to use the ancient Roman *mores* as the foundation of their dominion. The new masters were Christians, if Arian Christians, but their very insistence on the continuity of their rule with what had gone before automatically nourished the withering tissues of paganism, because the strongest, by far the strongest, single tenet in the pagan creed was the greatness and eternity of the great and Eternal City.

[1] Chapter XII.

Indeed, the very use of the word pagan is misleading. The word originally signified one who lives in a village, *pagus*, and so one who is separated from civilization, a rustic, in fact, and so it came to be used, in the first century A.D., to denote a civilian as distinguished from a soldier. Finally, by the days of Jerome and Augustine it had come to mean one who was neither Jewish nor Christian, and is so used in the legislation of Theodosius. But if a pagan of the fourth century had been asked what he thought of himself his first answer would have been that he regarded himself neither as a pagan nor as living in a fourth century: he was, he would have said, a supporter of orthodoxy, living in the eleventh century, that is the eleventh since the foundation of the City,[1] which had celebrated its millennium with great pomp in the days of Philip the Arabian. As a "good citizen" he would deplore the growth of a religion which had always, from its very birth, insisted that there must be another loyalty, not competitive, but supplementary, in addition to that felt towards the state. If men and women wanted something more personal than the traditional, corporate worship of the gods of Rome, then they could turn to the mystery religions which had for centuries been acclimatized in Rome. They could become followers of Isis, of Sarapis, of Mithras. Or they could adhere to the elevated and elevating philosophic systems of the Neoplatonists. It was quite unnecessary, indeed dangerous, to surrender to a faith which made demands on its adherents which might conflict with their duties to the state. Because it must be emphasized that the mystery religions did no such thing. They bestowed a sense of release, of spiritual euphoria; but they afforded no moral stimulus, no inducement to the living of a more abundant life. The Christian religion did, and in so doing might find itself in conflict with normal Roman practice, as for instance in the sphere of sexual morals or the games of the circus, the obscenities of the theatre or the resort to magic.

It is not to be supposed therefore that the Roman way of life was transmuted into a Christian profession in a generation. It

---

[1] Traditionally = 753 B.C. The system of chronology called the Era of the Incarnation was introduced by Dionysius Exiguus, a sixth-century canonist, who in writing of the dating of Easter, gives, as the birthday of Christ, the 25th March of the year 754 from the founding of Rome, which year thus becomes A.D. 1. (Dionysius got it wrong: how wrong has been a matter of long debate; but since we know that Herod the Great died in "4 B.C.", the discrepancy must be at least four years. It is in fact more probably five.)

I

never was, in a far more extended period, and the misunderstanding is really to be traced back to the life and policy of Constantine himself. For all too long the view prevailed that Constantine cynically "backed the winning horse" when he adopted and fostered the faith of the Christians, which had up to the time of his victory at the Milvian Bridge in 312, whereby he became master of Rome, been proscribed and persecuted. The truth is far otherwise. Constantine was convinced that he had been favoured by direct divine revelation, that he had been commanded to confide his arms and his fortune to the God of the Christians. He had done so, and that God had not failed him. For him, therefore, there could be no other god. By his patronage of the Church, by his personal efforts to promote its unity, he had shewn that he himself would like to see all men of his own way of thinking. But two aspects of the Constantinian "direction" in religious affairs must be borne in mind: first, that he used no coercion, and secondly, that his writ ran most strongly in the east, because it was in the east that he had established his new, and Christian, capital, and in the east that the new religion had originated and had spread most rapidly and widely. The west had produced splendid individual Christians, and so had Africa and Gaul; but the faith was far more thinly spread there than in the east. As the cleavage between east and west increased, so did the influence of the east upon the west weaken. At the council of Nicaea, at which Constantine presided in the year 325 with the object of settling the Arian question, the great majority of the close on 300 bishops came from the east: Britain and Illyricum sent none at all, Africa, Spain, Gaul and Dacia one each. Only one bishop came even from Italy, and the bishop of Rome was represented merely by two presbyters. And this at a time when the Church had actually outgrown the empire, territorially speaking, for there were bishops present from the Crimea, Persia, Armenia and the Gothic lands beyond the Danube.[1]

The tone of Roman society therefore remained largely, predominantly, pagan throughout the fourth century, and well into the fifth. "Many a literary noble of Aquitaine in the fifth century was probably as really pagan as the peasant who bowed before the old altar on Mount Eryx. His grandfather in the days of Ausonius [c. 310–c. 384] may have conformed to Christianity; some of his friends might have sold their lands, and followed S. Paulinus to Nola or S. Jerome to Bethlehem;

---

[1] *Cambridge Medieval History*, I, p. 13.

but he himself was often as little of a Christian as the men who, three generations before him, had pleaded with the Emperor to leave the Altar of Victory in the Senate-house. Like Ausonius, he might pay a cold and perfunctory homage to Christ, and visit the neighbouring town for the Easter festival; but the whole tone of his thoughts was inspired by the memories of the heathen past."[1] The dispute over the Altar of Victory, mentioned in this citation, is typical of the relations between Christians and pagans, of their relative influence, of their mutual relationships and of the efficacy of the laws proscribing pagan practices.

From the days of Augustus, a figure of Victory, brought originally from Tarentum, had stood in the Curia, or senate-house, down in the Forum, hard by the reputed tomb of Romulus himself.[2] Each senator, as he entered, was by ancient custom required to offer a pinch of incense to this venerable image,[3] which stood on a low pedestal at the end of the chamber opposite to the entrance. The salutation of the goddess was thus an act of public and personal recognition. Christian senators understandably abstained from any such compromise; it may therefore be wondered why they wished to deny the same latitude to their pagan confrères. At first sight it seems unreasonable, but we must remember that it was precisely this offering of incense to the deities of Rome which had been made the touchstone of a man's acceptance or rejection of Christianity from the very earliest days. Refusal to conform in this apparently trivial ceremony had cost countless loyal Christians their lives. To find the ritual still observed in the most solemn assembly of the City naturally irked them.

For a long time they kept silent, because the policy of Constantine and his successors had been in practice, as regarded the west, one of toleration. For twenty years after the death of Julian the legal situation of paganism underwent

---

[1] *Roman Society in the Last Century of the Western Empire*, Samuel Dill, p. 6. This book first appeared in 1898. A second and revised edition was issued in 1910. It is still the best work in English on the subject.

[2] The building is still there. Traditionally founded by Tullius Hostilius, Rome's third king, in the seventh century B.C., it was restored by Sulla and then by Julius Caesar in the first, again by Diocletian in A.D. 283. In the seventh century A.D. it was transformed into a church dedicated to St Adrian. In 1937 it resumed its pristine aspect. The original bronze doors were transferred by Borromini to St John Lateran. The building was one of the most honoured and august in all Rome.

[3] *Herodian*, Bk V, v, 7. The pedestal still survives.

no change, except that Valentinian-and-Valens, reviving the ordinances of Constantine, forbade magic, astrology and nocturnal sacrifices. Even so, they were careful to add that "neither the taking of omens, nor in addition any religion authorized by the ancestors shall be regarded as having a criminal nature".[1] Between 356 and 381 the Code contains no law directed against public heathen rites. The pontifical college still met, the Vestal virgins still watched over their undying fire, the feast of the Great Mother was still solemnized. Gratian on his accession did not expressly outlaw heathen worship, but he gave a presage of his future attitude by declining the pontifical robes and the title *pontifex maximus*, which all his Christian predecessors had been willing to assume.[2] In the year 383, when he had been emperor for eight years,[3] he ordered the figure of Victory to be removed from the Curia. It had been removed once before, by Constantius, when he visited Rome in A.D. 357,[4] but Julian, who became emperor four years later, replaced, it, and it had been un-molested ever since. Whether through the benevolent neutral-ity of Gratian's predecessors the senate was now predominantly pagan is a question on which the available texts contradict each other: the balance seems to have been pretty even. At all events, the pagans felt strong enough to try to get the order reversed. So powerful, however, was the Christian opposition that the delegation which the pagans sent north to interview the emperor was not even admitted to his presence, Damasus the bishop of Rome having tipped off the even more influential Ambrose bishop of Milan.[5] This was a sad setback for the pagans; but they seemed to be vindicated when within the year Gratian fell by the hand of an assassin,[6] and Italy was

---

[1] *Theodosian Code*, IX, xvi, 7–10. The Theodosian Code was compiled in 438 by order of Theodosius II. It is a collection of imperial constitutions since the days of Constantine, and is invaluable as a source. It was drawn up in Constantinople, and accepted in the west. Though its reception in Rome seems to symbolize the connexion of East and West, "its issue never-theless marks an epoch in the separation of the two. After 438 the East and the West legislate independently." *Cambridge Medieval History*, I, p. 412, n.

[2] It is now the only imperial title used by the pope.

[3] The date is disputed. J.-R. Palanque, *Histoire de l'Église*, Vol. 3, p. 514, places the order in 382, in which year the dignity of *pontifex maximus* was finally suppressed.

[4] Symmachus, *Rel.* III, 6.

[5] Ambrose, *Letters* 17, 10. Ambrose is discussed in Chapter XI.

[6] p. 50 above.

devastated by famine. Thus heartened, the pagans made new head. In 384, in the first year of the reign of Valentinian, it was they who in the persons of Praetextatus as praetorian prefect and Symmachus as prefect of the city occupied the highest offices of state. Of these two men more will be said below: here it is only necessary to note that they were the fine flower of the old pagan aristocracy of Rome, and that Symmachus, in his capacity of *princeps senatus*, carried the highest possible authority when making representations to the emperor in matters relating to that body.

We possess both the petition of Symmachus and the two letters which Ambrose addressed to the young sovereign.[1] Symmachus' oration is of the utmost value, as being the last formal and official exposition of the proscribed cult. It is marked by two characteristics, a tolerant scepticism, and a proud and ardent conservatism. "Every nation," he says, "has its own gods and peculiar rites. The Great Mystery cannot be approached by one avenue alone. But use and wont count for much in giving authority to a religion. Leave us the symbol on which our oaths of allegiance have been sworn for so many generations. Leave us the system which has so long given prosperity to the State. A religion should be judged by its utility to the men who hold it. Years of famine have been the punishment of sacrilege. The treasury should not be replenished by the wealth of the sacred colleges, but by the spoils of the enemy."[2] Then the figure of Rome herself is presented, to beseech, in a passage of moving eloquence, that she may be suffered to continue in her ancient ways, that ancient faith which had vanquished the Gauls and subdued Hannibal. "*Reveremini annos meos*," she pleads, "reverence my years." According to St Ambrose, even the Christian members of the privy council were impressed by the eloquence of Symmachus, and Ambrose himself, an orator of the first rank, confesses his admiration for it. But once again, it was Ambrose who prevailed.

In 391 Symmachus had risen to the highest dignity open to a commoner – he was consul, and his kinsman Flavianus was praetorian prefect. Once more Symmachus was sent northwards to state the pagans' case; but Theodosius was by now wholly subject to Ambrose's direction. The venerable consul was escorted from the presence with scant dignity, hurried to a waiting carriage and only set down at the hundredth milestone

---

[1] Symmachus, *Rel.* 3; Ambrose, *Letters*, 17 and 18.
[2] Dill's translation.

from Milan. A fourth, and final, appeal was made the following year. Ambrose was absent in Vienne; but despite the seeming paramountcy of the pagan count Arbogast, the young Valentinian stood firm. A few days later he was dead, a martyr to Arbogast's resentful spite.[1] During the short ascendancy of the usurper Eugenius, Flavianus did succeed in getting the statue replaced, and Theodosius seems to have left it undisturbed.[2] Victory still appeared on the coins. But in fact these were irrelevant anachronisms. The "crowning mercy" of the Frigidus had sealed the doom of paganism as a creed or a cause. But three years before that decisive battle, ironically enough in the very year of Symmachus' consulship, the law was promulgated which finally outlawed pagan practices.[3] Within the city of Rome every act of pagan worship was forbidden. No sacrifice might be offered, no temple visited, no image venerated. Officials who condoned any breach of the law were to be heavily punished. During the following year further edicts extended the prohibitions, one of which incited the Christians of Alexandria to destroy the famous Sarapeum. Finally, on 8th November, 392, was issued the edict which was to be the death-warrant of paganism – that is to say of toleration and religious freedom.[4] Thereafter, throughout the whole of the empire, in no matter what place or circumstances, even in private, it was utterly forbidden to offer sacrifices, to honour the *lares* with fire or the *genii* with libations or the *penates* with incense, to worship idols or to raise altars of turf. Fines and confiscations would punish those who disobeyed.

As we have seen, this savage legislation provoked a reaction; but it could not last long. The victory of the Frigidus involved the eclipse, by slaughter or suicide, of all the proponents of reaction. "The victory of Theodosius marks the definitive overthrow of paganism. After his death, which followed hard on his triumph, there would still be legislation against pagan superstition: in the East, Arcadius would renew, in 395, the prohibitions of his father, before abolishing, in 396, all priestly exemptions and ordaining in 399 the demolition of rural shrines; in the West Honorius, in 407 and 415, would confiscate

---

[1] p. 50 above.
[2] This is the inference from two references in Claudian's poems: *Sixth consulship of Honorius*, line 597, and *Stilicho's consulship* III, line 204.
[3] Signed at Milan on 24th February, *Theodosian Code*, XVI, x, 10.
[4] *Theodosian Code*, XVI, x, 12.

all temple revenues and suppress all the ceremonies which were tainted with paganism. Under Theodosius II again imperial constitutions would enjoin the destruction 'of all sanctuaries, temples, buildings of idolatry, if any still remain intact' or would deal with pagans 'who might still exist, although there ought not to be any'. But the very terms employed make it clear that it is the liquidation of a defunct régime. The decisive date, in this case again, is to be found under the first Theodosius, who, completing the work of Gratian, broke every link with paganism and, without persecuting its devotees, has made of it a religion deprived of its secular privileges and finally even of its rights. Liberty of worship no longer exists for it. Henceforth the only legal religion is Christianity."[1] Constantine has not seldom been derided, by those who have not understood his spiritual development, for interested patronage of the Church, so as to soften it, to make it malleable, the more readily to be hammered into the instrument of his own secular ambitions. This charge cannot be sustained, as the history of Constantine and his successors shows: toleration had been the guiding principle down to the days of Theodosius. It is on Theodosius that must for ever lie the odium of having inflicted on mankind, yet again, in an epoch in which the Gospel of love was liberating more souls than ever before, the savage shackles of conformity. Religious intolerance there had been in days gone by, it had existed in Assyria, it had existed in Palestine; it had existed, in its most ferocious form, in the Roman dominions, and it was the Christians who had been its victims. But now, for close on a century, the equable toleration which was Constantine's most precious gift to his empire had been maintained. That it should have been ended by Theodosius is one of the tragedies of history.

To us, looking back over centuries of religious persecution, it is hard to see why this step should ever have been taken, because of pagan society as it was at the end of the fourth century, it is permissible to postulate two things without fear of contradiction; the first is that the line between it and Christian society was very lightly, not to say, vaguely drawn, and the second is that it was in any case doomed to extinction. But

---

[1] Palanque, *op. cit.*, p. 518, who notes that the Jews were expressly tolerated. Polygamy was forbidden to them, nor might they intermarry with Christians. But their worship was assured, their synagogues pronounced inviolate. Their clergy enjoyed the same exemption and privileges as the Christian priesthood.

it was these two very qualities that goaded Theodosius and those who thought like him to action. It was not desirable, in their pure view, that Christians should be "contaminated" by close association with the ungodly; and if the old way of life was moribund, surely it would be best to end it at once?

The dispute over the statue of Victory shews how closely pagan and Christian were associated in the public service. Ambrose and Symmachus could correspond in perfect amity: the question was debated with parliamentary decorum. It was the same in many walks of life. Marriages between Christians and pagans were common, so that members of the same family might belong to either group – camps they cannot be called, where there was so little rancour. Superficially, there was little to differentiate a Christian from a pagan. It is only when we examine the spiritual springs which animated them that we discover the fundamental difference. It so happens, rather pathetically, that we know more about society in the very last days of the empire than we know about it in any other period of its long life except the very first. We have, to name the secular writers only, the letters and speeches of Symmachus, the *Saturnalia* of Macrobius, in which Symmachus and his friends play so large a part, we have the poets Ausonius and Claudian. Ammianus has already been frequently mentioned. In the next century we have Rutilius Namatianus at the beginning and Sidonius Apollinaris at the end. Between them, these authorities furnish us with a vivid picture of the society of the age.

The outstanding quality, if such it may be called, the common denominator, of all these writers is a pathological nostalgia for the past. This was due in large measure no doubt to the education to which they had all been exposed, the training in "rhetoric" of which the object was to produce an orator who could speak on any topic, without hesitation and without conviction. All the old myths of Greece, all the old glories of Rome, back they went to them, these polished hacks, over and over again. The present, as an intellectual environment, meant but little to them, the future nothing at all. It must be emphasized that Christians no less than pagans were subjected to this stunting curriculum, which makes the courage and vision of those who survived it all the more remarkable.

"Whatever the salient characteristics of the fourth century may be, intellectual freshness, imagination and a broad human outlook are not amongst them. The old literary forms and

methods were outworn, and there was no spiritual force to
reanimate or to reshape them. The accessible realms of the
intellect had been delimited, mapped out, and explored as
definitely as the Roman empire itself; and outside (it was now
tacitly assumed) was nothing but chaos, just as beyond the
political and military frontiers of the state lay nothing but
barbarism."[1]

Macrobius, in his *Saturnalia*, admits us to the company of
the leading men of the Rome of his day. We assemble in the
house of Praetextatus, scholar, statesman, philosopher and
antiquary, former prefect of the City and governor of Greece,
an adept, too, of half a dozen mysteries. He is the ideal
president for such an assembly. Then there is the great Symmachus himself. There are two members of the Albini family,
ardent Virgilians both. There is a doctor called Disarius, who
is a friend of St Ambrose. Horus, evidently an Egyptian,
Servius, a youthful scholar, and Evangelus, a boor introduced
as a foil to the others, make up the number. All these were real
people. What do they talk about? Antiquities of course, the
origin of the calendar, of the Saturnalia itself, of the broad-
striped toga, worn by children and magistrates.[2] Literature
means for these men chiefly Cicero and Virgil, who had
flourished more than four centuries earlier. Medicine, astro-
nomy, philosophy and ethics, etiquette and famous sayings
fill in the time. The philosophy is an eclectic farrago of various
cults, the philosophy largely Stoic, with discussions of the
old threadbare topics, slavery and suicide.

Of Christianity there is no mention whatever. Yet one of
the Albini had a Christian wife, the other was almost certainly
himself a Christian. It is the same in real life. Symmachus,
in the whole range of his private letters, speaks but rarely of
religion, never once of Christianity. It is the same with the
poets and the panegyrists. They seem to have agreed, these
great Roman nobles, to ignore the new faith. The old was good
enough for them. Old books, old ideas, old creeds.

Ausonius was highly regarded by his contemporaries;
Symmachus compares his poem on the Moselle (which Alexander Pope found worthy of adaptation) to the work of Virgil,
his pupil Paulinus of Nola considers him as being at least the

---

[1] Hugh G. Evelyn White, Introduction to *Ausonius*, Loeb Edn., p. xxv.
[2] As so often, the use of the Roman Church perpetuates that of the empire. Here the analogue is the coloured cassock, worn by seminarians and
porporati alike.

equal of Cicero and Virgil. Down to our own times, Ausonius has been judged largely on his one famous poem. This is unfair: the bulk of his work is greatly inferior. Gibbon's remark that "the poetical fame of Ausonius condemns the taste of his age" is a juster verdict.[1] He, too, was a product of the petrified instruction of his age. The treasures of ancient literature were valued not for their spirit, but for their form, not for the thought, but for the way the words were used. Eloquence was held to consist not in the statement of a fact, but in the production of an effect.

Thus we find that "from first to last Ausonius' verse is wholly barren of ideas: not a gleam of insight or of broad human sympathy, no passion, no revolt: his attitude towards life is a mechanical and complacent acceptance of things as they are".[2]

With Claudian we fare little better. Triviality, obscurity, verbosity cloud and retard his rhythm. His "conceits" are narcotic. To cite but one: in his invective against Rufinus, which is stuffed with antiquarian allusions, inflated with hyperbole and made tedious with insincerity, Claudian comes at last to Rufinus' death. As related on p. 53, Rufinus had been murdered at the instigation of Stilicho. He had in fact been torn limb from limb by the soldiers. Claudian must make this the occasion for a show-off of his ingenuity, so he says that Rufinus was "*nusquam totiensque sepultus*", "never, yet so many times, buried". Claudian could devote no less than seven little poems to one drop of water enclosed in a piece of rock-crystal.

To dilate further upon the desiccated banality of these virtuosi of the dusk would be to inflict the tedium for which they are blamed. We must pass on to the very last of them, Sidonius Apollinaris, poet and bishop. Sidonius is of great value as a source of information about how in the twilight of the fifth century the nobles of southern Gaul and their friends still contrived to live *La Dolce Vita*, "rich men furnished with ability, living peaceably in their habitations", or as peaceably as the disturbed times would allow. Much of our knowledge of the secular life of the age, of the relations between Roman and barbarian, is drawn from the letters and poems of Sidonius. For instance, his poem on the *Burgus*, or castle,[3] of Pontius

---

[1] Ed. Bury, III, p. 134, n. 1.

[2] White, *op. cit.*, p. xxvi.

[3] From the Greek *Pyrgos*; cf. our cognate place-name Burgh.

Leontius, barnacled as it is with mythological allusions, does nevertheless give us a description of a feudal château of the late fifth century, near the confluence of the Garonne and Dordogne which is comparable to Pliny's famous description of his villa, and is a vivid commentary on the famous mosaics of Carthage and Sousse. For the rest, his style is vitiated by the faults already noticed. The best verdict on Sidonius is probably that of Hodgkin. On 13th November, 1878, he wrote: "I have to finish off the letters and poems of Sidonius Apollinaris as the time has come for writing a chapter about him in my history.

"The chapter is to be headed 'Sidonius, or Verses by a Person of Quality'.[1] He is just the sort of man with whom I have least patience, flaccid, bombastic, conceited – and a member of a large and extraordinarily foolish Mutual Flattery Society, but he is the one man who really tells us anything about the inner life of the Western empire during the last quarter of a century of its existence."

Claudian appears to have fallen from favour after the death of Stilicho, whose panegyrist he had been. A few years later, we catch sight for all too brief a moment of the last genuine pagan Latin poet, Rutilius Namatianus, whose fragmentary description of a journey from Rome to his home in Gaul has aptly been called by his Loeb editor "the swan-song of Rome". Namatianus detested Stilicho: he was a Roman with all the provincial's ardour; and his sentimental optimism, his blind belief in Rome's greatness and eternity have already been mentioned.[2] His description of the Roman countryside as it was in the autumn of the year 416 is of great interest. But what is of chief value for the purpose of the present study is Namatianus' attitude to antiquity and to the disturbing novelty, as it was to him, of Christianity. Namatianus was a friend of Albinus, whom he addresses in terms of affectionate admiration: Albinus had been his successor in the exalted office of prefect of the City; but to the Christians in general, indeed to any enemy of paganism, he is uncompromisingly hostile. Stilicho, the man who burned the Sibylline books, is bidden to replace Nero in the depths of Tartarus: Nero destroyed only his own mother, Stilicho the mother of the world, by allowing

---

[1] As published, Chapter III of Book 3, it is headed simply "The Letters and Poems of Apollinaris Sidonius". The letter is quoted from *The Life and Letters of Thomas Hodgkin*, by Louise Creighton, 1917.

[2] p. 66 above.

the barbarians to enter Italy.[1] He loathes the Jews,[2] and pours contempt upon the ascetic monks whom he encountered in the island of Capraria.[3] In Dill's view, "that such a poem should have been published under the Christian empire, and that its author should have held the highest office, is startling proof of the persistence of the old Roman practical toleration of freedom of thought. Rutilius had little conception of the force and destiny of the movement which he derided."[4]

If from literature we turn to the arts of architecture, sculpture and decoration we observe the same general pattern – a pathetic regard for antiquity combined with an ever-lessening life in its transmission. The decline set in at the beginning of the fourth century, if not before. It is illustrated in monuments familiar to every Mediterranean traveller. The sculptures of the Arch of Constantine in Rome are probably the best known example. The finest of them are taken from structures dedicated to Trajan, Hadrian and Marcus Aurelius. To compare these with the work executed expressly for the Arch itself, in the year 315, is to be struck most dolefully by its degeneracy. The same feeling of a lack, of something ravished, strikes the beholder as he gazes upon the almost brutish faces of the famous Tetrarchs which stand at the entrance to the Doges' Palace at Venice. Bernard Berenson has this to say of them: "These portraits are full length in porphyry. The material offered no difficulties, for its resistances had been overcome generations ago and it was worked with the ease of any other marble or stone then in use. Nor can it be said that the specific qualities of porphyry were respected in these effigies as they were so admirably and signally in the mighty sarcophagus of Constantia now in the Vatican.

"Their strangeness as works of art in a period still antique is thus not due to their material but to the visual concept of the sculptor or sculptors who made them. It is a concept so mediaeval that as regards the Venetian group I can seldom get over the impression that they are somewhat orientalized crusaders, Knights Templars, let us say, imparting the kiss of peace. Their caps, their cloaks, their tunics, their belts, the pommels of their swords, their scabbards have nothing about them to recall Roman warriors, let alone emperors and their successors designate. Nor is there anything in their physique, in their proportions, in their facial types with wrinkled foreheads and

[1] II, 41.   [2] I, 384–398.   [3] I, 440.
[4] Dill, op. cit., pp. 47 and 48.

all but simian profiles, nor in their actions, to recall the majesty of the Augusti and Caesars of Imperial Rome."[1]

And yet the tough, tenacious old Roman spirit lived on, in architecture as it did in literature. The church of Santa Costanza, which is roughly contemporary with the Tetrarchs, really sums up the whole argument of this chapter. That building, designed originally to be the mausoleum of Constantia, or Constantina, the daughter of Constantine, may well be regarded as the last "Roman" edifice. It shews the Roman mastery of space, the Roman virtuosity in vaulting, the Roman "gravitas" and proportion at their classical best. On the ceilings are pretty little pagan *putti*, rendered in the same lively mosaic as formerly adorned secular floors. And yet the whole is Christian in feeling and design. This building is no piece of antiquarian "in keeping" – it has a definite personality of its own. You do not feel, when meditating in the church of Santa Costanza, that you are bidding farewell to a dying tradition (as you do when you read the pages of the poets mentioned above, or when you behold the sculptures just referred to); you feel that you are equipped with all that the traditional genius of Rome can bestow upon you, and that, so endowed, you are about to set out on a journey, a pilgrimage into a new epoch.

That is exactly what the Christian leaders of the age felt themselves. It will now be appropriate to examine a few of them.

---

[1] *The Arch of Constantine: The Decline of Form*, Bernard Berenson, 1952, pp. 48 and 49. The whole of this little work – the first chapter of a larger book which was never written – is worth careful study.

CHAPTER X

THE NEW WORLD

As mentioned in the last chapter, Sidonius Apollinaris became a bishop: in 471 we find him enthroned at Clermont, having apparently been consecrated the year before. This transformation may cause us some surprise. That a Gallo-Roman nobleman, the son-in-law of the emperor Avitus, to whom, as to two others, Majorian and Anthemius, he had delivered public panegyrics, the man who had become city prefect and president of the senate, the feudal lord and poet – that such a man should abandon all the pomps of this world in order to promote the glories of the next, must strike us as bewildering indeed. And yet it was a symptom, a dramatic demonstration, of the changing values of the age.

Sidonius was not the first secular star to enter the spiritual orbit. His own father-in-law, after his defeat by Ricimer in 456, had been compulsorily consecrated: so had Glycerius in similar case eighteen years later. Even the great Ambrose himself, as we shall see, had progressed from governor to bishop in a week. But the case of Sidonius is of particular interest. Ambrose had been elected by popular acclaim; for Avitus and Glycerius their mitres had in effect served as extinguishers; but Sidonius was to demonstrate that however despicable he might have been as a poet, as a bishop he was to prove himself capable, courageous and steadfast. Why did he make this change? Sidonius loved Rome: to be constrained to witness the progressive disintegration of its greatness was hard indeed for so loyal a spirit. But how could he help to arrest it? As the secular power declined, it was the Church that shewed itself stable, immutable and the giver of life. And the bishops were the very embodiment of that life. They had for long been the champions of their flocks against oppression, whether by rapacious officials or barbarian aggressors. The bishop had for long been invested with certain judicial authority. He was the steward of considerable financial resources. Above all, he was a member of a disciplined society, whose aims were known and constant, whose hierarchy looked to one head whose authority was unchallenged, in marked contrast to the cascade of competitors which surged over the secular scene. Worldly power might oscillate between Milan and Constantinople, Trier and Ravenna, but for the Christian Church, Rome and Rome alone had long been paramount. Her jurisdiction had spread gradually, first over the congregations and sees of Italy, of which by the middle of the third century her bishop was the acknowledged metropolitan. This authority had become ever more widely diffused, apart altogether from the moral prestige which the Roman see enjoyed as being the only one which had been founded not by one Apostle only but by two, Peter and Paul, and that in the capital of the known world. The primacy of Rome was, as has been well said, "felt before it was defined". Not even a prelate of the stature of Ambrose challenged it. By the end of the fourth century it was firmly established. And not only in ecclesiastical matters. Ever since the day when Leo had confronted Attila it had been clear to all that it was the Church which now enjoyed the initiative in secular affairs no less than spiritual ones.[1]

The Visigothic king, Euric, was an Arian, an ardent opponent of Catholicism. It needed a man of Sidonius's stature to stand up to him. The new prelate was no theologian; but he was a man of simple devotion, integrity and loyalty. What a change his new vocation had wrought in the facile and vapid verse-maker! He even resolved to write no more worldly verse[2] though he can still, even when discussing the most serious topics, indulge in maddening "conceits". Here is an example: Sidonius is writing to his brother-in-law Ecdicius, who had shewn outstanding gallantry in resisting the Gothic raids on Auvergne, despite the treachery of the Roman governor Seronatus. "Your countrymen the Arverni have now to bear two troubles at once. 'What can they be?' you ask. Seronatus' presence and your absence. Seronatus', I say, whose very name, I may remark at the outset, makes me feel that chance, foreseeing the future, must have played a joke, just as our ancestors, going by contraries, called wars, which are the foulest of all things, *bella* [beautiful] and with like contradiction called the Fates *Parcae*, because they spared not [*parcere*]. This very Catiline of our age returned lately from Aire to make one big draught of the blood and the fortunes of the wretched inhabitants, after a good taste of such

---

[1] For the development of the papal primacy see Palanque, *op. cit.*, Chapter IV, pp. 447 *seq.*

[2] *Letters*, IX, 12, 1.

refreshment in the other place."[1] One wonders how, with such a stylist at the helm, anything ever got done. But we must not be too hard on poor Sidonius. He was in fact so zealous in his promotion of Romanism that, when Auvergne was finally ceded to the Goths in 475, he was imprisoned in a fortress near Carcassonne. He was released the next year, and retired to Bordeaux. Within the decade – we do not know just when – he was dead. He was canonized, and the feast of St Sidonius is still celebrated at Clermont on 21st August.

Sidonius is by no means the only one of his kind. There was St Paulinus of Nola, a friend of St Augustine. A native of Bordeaux, a member of the great Anician family, and a pupil of Ausonius, Paulinus became consul and then governor of Campania. He was only twenty-five. Feeling that God had need of him, he sold his patrimony in Aquitaine, became bishop of Nola, and turned his secular experience of government to good account in the administration of his diocese. He, too, withstood Alaric, and died of his sufferings of body and spirit in the following year. He was a poet of sincerity and charm. St Hilary of Arles was a bishop at the age of thirty in 428, St Eucherius of Lyons consecrated in 434 had been a senator; and there were many more who as churchmen and Romans defended Church and state – to them indivisible.[2]

Besides the bishops, there was another great source of power at the disposal of the Church – monasticism. No flowering of the many-splendoured Christian genius caused more controversy for longer than the monastic movement. Men are born lonely; lonely, they know, they will die – *"On mourra seul"*. They do not care therefore to see their brethren withdraw from human society and thereby make life more lonely still. That is the root of the ordinary mortal's instinctive resentment of those who lead the solitary or segregated life; but this resentment is greatly increased by the startling discovery that men and women who live their lives by a strict rule, in separated communities, are generally more serene, often more productive, than their secular fellows. Resentment may thus melt into admiration, admiration crystallize into a resolve to imitate.

The monastic movement was the product of the east and of the desert. From the days of Moses to those of Muhammad, the desert was to be the nursery of souls. Jesus had retired to

[1] *Ibid.*, II, I, 1 (tr. Anderson, Loeb edn.).
[2] Daniel-Rops has some valuable pages on these heroes: *The Church in the Dark Ages*, pp. 80 *seq.*

the desert, so had St Paul. There is something compelling about those almost lunar spaces, an influence that seems to calcine the material attributes of a man to the same consistency as the landscape over which he wanders, so that human pride and diversity are burned away and only divine unity left for contemplation. The ascetic[1] strain was present in the Christian conception of life from the beginning. It was preached by Jesus, elaborated by St Paul. Celibacy was the first and remained the chief asceticism. Female ascetics were early recognized, virgins and widows being regarded almost as members of what would later be "orders". In the Life of St Antony we read that he placed his sister in a *Parthenon*, which later came to mean a nunnery. The women were organized before the men, who at this period merely retired individually to live in huts on the outskirts of the towns. And this is what St Antony did when he decided to leave the world.

St Antony was born in Egypt about the middle of the third century. When he was twenty he heard one day in church the words of the Gospel "If thou wilt be perfect, go and sell that thou hast, and give to the poor . . . and come and follow me".[2] It was, he felt, a personal call, obeying which he went to dwell with the ascetics who lived near his native town. After fifteen years so spent, he decided that he must seek absolute solitude, and so, in or about 285, he withdrew to a place called Pispir, now Deir-el-Maimūn, on the east bank of the Nile, opposite the Fayyūm. Here he lived in complete seclusion for another twenty years, spent wholly in prayer and spiritual exercises. The fame of his sanctity spread far and wide, and numbers of would-be ascetics gathered around him. Finally yielding to their insistence, he emerged from his solitude and became the first organizer of a Christian monastic community. This occurred, according to tradition, in the year 305.

The form of monachism inspired by St Antony spread throughout northern Egypt. Its leading feature, as we learn from Palladius, was its voluntariness. Some men lived as hermits, out of sight or sound of each other, assembling only for services on Saturdays and Sundays. Other monks, such as those in the still-famous Wady Natrūn, just south of the main Alexandria–Cairo road, lived as a community, and engaged in useful labour, as bakers, weavers and gardeners, or as

[1] The Greek word *askēsis* simply meant originally athletic training.
[2] *Matthew* XIX, 21.

K

physicians. But always these monks, even in the great settlements of Wady Natrūn and Scete, retained something of the hermetic life.[1]

The same Palladius, to whom we owe our picture of the Antonian settlements as they were in the year 390, has also described for us the more gregarious and disciplined variant from which western monachism was to develop. This owed its origin to a certain Pachomius. Born a pagan, Pachomius became a Christian at the age of twenty. An angel, it was said, had appeared to him as he sat alone in his cave, bidding him come forth and do for others what he had done for himself, that is, organize the holy life for them. So handing him a brazen tablet on which was inscribed the Rule, the angel commanded him to gather together all the young monks in the vicinity, and to become their leader. Thus it came about that Pachomius founded his first monastery at Tabennisi near Denderah, in southern Egypt, in the second decade of the fourth century. When he died in 346 no less than 3,000 monks, disposed in nine monasteries, had adopted the Pachomian rule. There was, too, one house for women. By the end of the century, Palladius says, there were 7,000 Pachomian monks.

Palladius' account of the daily life at the monastery of Panopolis (Akhmīm) is of living interest. Three hundred monks dwelt there, working as artificers of all kinds, and contributing to the maintenance of nunneries and prisons. Those who were on the weekly roster of servers rose at dawn, and while some were busy in the kitchen, others laid the tables, putting out bread, mustard leaves, olive salad, cheese, chopped herbs, just as would be found to-day. For the old and infirm a little meat was provided. "Some come in to eat at noon, others at one, or two, or three or five, or in the late evening, and others every second day. Their work was similarly distributed: one worked in the fields, another in the garden, another in the smithy, another in the bakery, another at carpentry, another at fulling, another at basket-making, another in the tanyard, another at shoe-making, another at tailoring, another at calligraphy."[2] The monks also kept pigs

---

[1] The word *scete* is still in use on Mount Athos, to denote a detached monastic dwelling. Indeed, after 1,500 years the religious life of the Holy Mountain retains a surprising number of Antonian characteristics, specially its leaving to the individual the choice of what degree of solitude he is to adopt.

[2] Quoted by Dom E. C. Butler, Abbot of Downside Abbey, in *Cambridge Medieval History*, Vol. 1, p. 524.

and camels. They assembled for worship four times a day, took Communion on Saturdays and Sundays, and knew the Scriptures by heart.

Thus, at the very outset of the monastic movement we can discern the differences between east and west which have lasted down to our own day. That the eastern type of monastic life laid more stress on contemplation than on manual work (which was subordinate and incidental) is undeniable. Equally certain is it that it could and did lend itself to extravagances. It was therefore perhaps unfortunate that it was the eastern variety of monachism which was the first to reach the west. Not that contemplation is an experience unknown to the west; but it must be admitted that for the average westerner Martha is a secret saint: we admire "action", we respect "results". It is this attitude which led Rutilius to misprise the monks of Capraria, just as nowadays it leads to the "What good do they do?" attitude of certain western visitors to Mount Athos or the Meteora. To the eastern spirit being is often more important, because more actual, than doing.

This distrust of the monastic vocation led to another common criticism of them – that they deprived the state of so many valuable brains and bodies that they were largely responsible for its impending ruin. They were worthless, these monks, so ran the argument, and at the same time priceless, idle yet active, vain yet vigorous. To anyone who attempts to calculate what civilization owes to the monasteries, this line of reasoning, if such it can be called, seems silly. It is indeed appalling to think how little of antiquity would be known to us from written sources but for the manuscripts which were for centuries preserved and copied in Christian monasteries. But not only did the monasteries preserve literature; they also provided leaders, those very men that their secular critics craved, the hero-bishops.

Eastern monachism received its definitive form from St Basil, who lived during the latter part of the fourth century. Retiring to a lonely retreat in Pontus in what is now northern Turkey, St Basil worked out the ideal of the monastic life which is still the rule not only in the east but largely in the west as well, because St Benedict based his own rule on the same principles. St Basil's underlying injunction was unity. Whereas the Pachomians might live in different houses and do different things at different times, the Basilians must live under the same roof, eat together and worship together. Secondly,

St Basil ordained that monks must seek the advantage not merely of their own souls (as the hermits did) but of their fellow men. Orphanages and schools were attached to the monasteries; and ascetic rigours must not be practised to the detriment of work. Nor might his monks wander: they must continue in the house of their first vocation.

That many sought the monastic life as a refuge from the world there is no doubt. The world they left was not only moribund but corrupt, almost inescapably so. Vices, like other aspects of behaviour, have their vogues. During the nineteenth century it was the sexual licence of the ancients which came in for the sharpest slaps. During the twentieth the emphasis has tended to shift towards the inhumanity of Roman life, its tortures, burnings, delight in the destruction of life, both of men and of animals, as an amusement, an escape from the boredom of a life which was wholly exempt from the slightest intellectual enterprise, even of the need to earn a living. Both aspects were abundantly harassing. What a contrast is to be found in the busy, virile, thinking, clean and generous life of the monasteries.

It was St Benedict who, in the early part of the sixth century, founded his famous monastery of Monte Cassino, and so provided the western church with the monastic pattern it was to preserve for almost seven centuries; but great monastic centres existed long before his time, both in the east and the west. *A Little Rule for Beginners* is the modest title he gives to the most influential programme for life ever formulated.

Bishops and monks: it was these men who were to preserve the old and to forge the new. Not everyone by any means favoured their pre-eminence. To-day we commend Sidonius for his courage, while we deplore his poems. His contemporaries, many of them, took an exactly opposite view. Similarly, while we praise the monks for having been the agents for the preservation of our classical heritage, the men among whom they lived blamed them for hastening its destruction. It was by no means a foregone conclusion that the episcopate would assume in the Christian world the task which Prometheus had undertaken in the pagan – the transmission of the sacred, vivifying spark; nor yet that monks and nuns, diffused as they were in many parts of the empire and speaking and writing different tongues, should become the united kingdom of God which they did in fact constitute and still do.

That this was in fact the result, and that the old to this day lives in the new, is largely the work of three great men. Each of them has already been mentioned in this narrative. They were men of different origins, different methods, different talents. Yet they were all three to be connected in the building of the same golden bridge. Their names were Ambrose, Jerome and Augustine.

CHAPTER XI

THE STRONG MEN

While it is true that Ambrose, Jerome and Augustine were men of very different natures, characters and achievements, they all had two qualities in common: freedom from fear and certainty of aim.

It is hard for us nowadays to realize how obedient to terror every ordinary pagan was throughout his days. High or low, emperor or peasant, he lived each day in a state of nervous wonder as to what fate might inflict upon him, and not only fate – the magical contrivances of his enemies as well. The state, indeed, recognized the paramount influence of omens. No important project could be undertaken unless the auspices, as revealed by the flight of birds or the entrails of animals, were favourable: our very word *inaugurate* perpetuates this attitude of mind. Generals would trust soothsayers rather than strategists; emperors were guided by the colour of a chicken's liver. The authors of the so-called *Augustan History*, a series of biographies ranging from Hadrian to the early days of Diocletian, continually pepper their narratives with prodigies, to which, it is clear, they attached a factual importance. Here, for instance, is the passage which tells of the signs which foretold the elevation of Tacitus (275–276), chosen for its moderation – there are no two-headed calves or other monstrosities in it, just straightforward soothsaying.[1]

"The omens that predicted the rule of Tacitus were the following: A certain madman in the temple of Silvanus was seized with a stiffening of the limbs and shouted out, 'there is tacit purple, there is tacit purple', and so on for seven times; and this indeed was later regarded as an omen. The wine, moreover, with which Tacitus was about to pour a libation in the temple of Hercules Fundanius suddenly turned purple, and a vine which had previously borne white Amminian grapes in the year in which he gained the imperial power bore grapes of a purple colour. Very many other things turned purple. Now the omens predicting his death were these: His father's tomb burst its doors asunder and opened of its own

[1] *Augustan History*, Tacitus XVII, 1–5; tr. Loeb.

accord. His mother's shade appeared in the daytime as though alive to Tacitus and to Florian as well – it is indeed said that they had different fathers. All the gods in their private chapel fell down, overthrown either by an earthquake or by some mischance. The statue of Apollo, worshipped by them both, was found removed from the top of its pedestal and laid on a couch, without the agency of any human hand."

All of which sounds comparatively harmless. But although it is tolerably easy to tell white from black, light from darkness, it is often extremely hard to define the line that divides them: in a world where such beliefs flourished, evil arts and magical practices proliferated too. Every Roman was afraid of them. A famous but almost certainly unauthentic letter of the emperor Hadrian[1] to his brother-in-law, talking of Egypt, says that in that country everyone is addicted to magic. "There is no chief of the Jewish synagogue, no Samaritan, no Christian presbyter, who is not an astrologer, a soothsayer, or an anointer." We learn a great deal of the spread of such arts and of the terror they instilled from the pages of Ammianus. The emperor Valens (364–378) had a pathological fear of magic, and instituted a grand witch-hunt. It came to his ears that two men skilled in divination, one of whom had served in the household troops, had forecast that Valens would be succeeded by an excellent prince, and that the enquirers would come to a sad end. When they were arrested they admitted under torture that they had used the equivalent of an ouija-board, which had spelled out the letters THEOD. The enquirers took this to refer to a certain Theodore, an imperial secretary of excellent character. Everyone connected with the séance, including Theodore himself, was arrested, tortured and executed.[2] "Then," says Ammianus, "innumerable writings and many stocks of volumes were hauled out from various houses and under the eyes of the judges were burned in heaps as being unlawful, to allay the indignation at the executions, although the greater number were treatises on the liberal arts and on jurisprudence". "As a result," he adds a little farther on,[3] "throughout the oriental provinces owners of

---

[1] *Augustan History, Firmus*, etc., VIII, 1. The Latin words are: ". . . *non mathematicus, non haruspex, non aliptes*".

[2] The story of this *cause célèbre*, including details of the apparatus used by the enquirers, is given by Ammianus, Book XXIX, 1, 5 *seq.* The prediction could apply equally to Theodosius, who did, in fact, succeed.

[3] XXIX, 2, 4.

books, through fear of a like fate, burned their entire libraries; so great was the terror that had seized them all." In this way Valens deprived us of a large store of literature, in particular of the works of the philosophers.

The strangest, and in a way, the saddest, testimony to the belief in magic comes from the level-headed Ammianus himself. He tells us that a certain Faustinus, a state secretary, was tortured and put to death on the charge of having killed a donkey for use in some magical rite, whereas, says Ammianus, he had in fact merely wanted to use it to strengthen his hair, which was falling out.[1]

From this crepuscular mumbo-jumbo, with all its terrors and savage penalties, the Christian was liberated: the truth, as St Paul had been the first to point out, had made him free. That in itself gave him a great reserve of strength. But he possessed another, more positive asset. The Christian, even an Arian Christian, knew exactly and precisely what he believed. The great Christological controversies of the fourth and fifth centuries lie outside the scope of this study – they were nearly all centred in the east rather than in the west, and do not directly concern the subject of this enquiry. But of their outcome this must be said: by the end of the fifth century, as the result of Councils, aided by imperial ordinances, the nature of Christ, the will of Christ, the nature of the Trinity, the relationship of the Virgin Mary to her Son, man's will and destiny – all these and more had been settled, after long and often acrimonious discussion. It is as easy as it is foolish to pour scorn on the minutiae (as they seemed) that divided the opposing disputants. To "the half-believer in his casual creed" such matters may seem irrelevant. To the Christian of the day they were vital. He must be intellectually, as well as morally, certain that his faith was founded on the best and surest foundations of reason. It is also not inappropriate to recall that in the course of these investigations, the theologians of the fourth and fifth centuries contributed more to our knowledge of personality and what constitutes it than any other philosophers before the rise of the modern school of psychologists.

We may now briefly examine this fixity of mind and purpose in action.

In the year 373 the city of Milan was in an uproar. The bishop had died, and the Catholic and Arian parties were at

---

[1] XXX, 5, 11. For the use of donkeys and other animals in medicine, see Pliny, *Natural History*, XXVIII, p. 180.

each others' throats, each determined that the new prelate should be of their persuasion. The civil governor responsible for the maintenance of order was the *consularis* of Aemilia and Liguria, a man of about thirty-four, the son of a praetorian prefect of Gaul.[1] His name was Ambrose. By a fortunate chance, we know what he looked like, which can be said of no other of his peers. In his church at Milan there is a mosaic portrait of him, and beneath it the actual skeleton of Ambrose, which came to light when his tomb was opened in 1871. As Achilles Ratti (afterwards Pope Pius XI) pointed out in 1897, the portrait and the skeleton tally, even in details: for instance, one eye is lower than the other in each case. Ambrose was short, only 1·63 metres or a little over 5 feet in height, with a high forehead, big eyes and a firm chin. He has the prominent mouth of the orator. His feet and hands are delicate.

When he strode into the cathedral, to quell the hubbub, a child, it is said, called out "Ambrose for bishop". At once the cry was taken up. In vain did Ambrose protest that he had not even been baptized, that he was but a catechumen. The citizens would accept no excuses; and within a week, Ambrose was transformed from postulant to prelate, from governor to metropolitan. From the moment of his assumption of the mitre, Ambrose shewed himself a staunch and courageous Christian leader. Milan had recently become the residence of the emperor, a distinction it was to enjoy until 404, when Honorius retired to Ravenna. It was therefore for all practical purposes the capital of the west, and Ambrose enjoyed a prestige almost equal to that of the bishop of Rome. This he was careful not to infringe; but when he promulgated a decision taken by the pope, he did so by the authority of a synod summoned by himself.

Ambrose went further: not only did he claim and exercise metropolitan authority over the Church in the north, he insisted that even the emperor must bow to his direction in matters spiritual. Valentinian II, for his part, relied on Ambrose for secular counsel: he twice employed him, in 383 and 386, as an ambassador to Maximus, the usurper who had occupied nearly all of Gaul and threatened to invade Italy. These missions even enjoyed the approval of Justina, Valentinian's Arian mother, who disputed with Ambrose the guidance

---

[1] For date and age I follow Palanque, *op. cit.*, p. 472. The *Cambridge Medieval History*, Vol. I, p. 239, places his election in 374 and makes him about thirty-seven.

of her young son. Her influence was politically disastrous, because, at a time when Valentinian had preferred her counsel to that of the orthodox bishop, in 387, Maximus could pose as the Catholic champion, and in that specious guise invaded Italy. It needed the intervention of Theodosius, who had recently married Valentinian's sister, to bring about the downfall of Maximus. With Justina's death, in the following year, Valentinian's conversion to orthodoxy was assured.

Two years before that time, Justina's factious intrigues had produced a result which she can hardly have foreseen or intended. Her troops had surrounded the Porcian basilica, inside which Ambrose was ministering to his Catholic flock. The worshippers realized that they were besieged, and naturally enough they became more and more terrified. To calm them, and to keep them occupied, Ambrose hit on the idea of dividing them into two choirs, and making them sing hymns and psalms in turn. Ambrose was not the first to adopt this form of community singing. It had been invented in Antioch about the middle of the fourth century, whence it spread over the east, not without meeting opposition, as every ecclesiastical innovation must. It was Ambrose who introduced it to the west. The effect was remarkable. "People say," reported Ambrose,[1] "that I have bewitched the people with the verses of my hymns. I don't deny it. I have there a fine incantation, more potent than any other. What can be more potent than the confession of the Trinity, intoned each day by the voice of a whole people? They all vie with each other in proclaiming their faith. They have learned to celebrate in verse the Father, the Son and the Holy Spirit. And thus have become past masters the very folk who only just managed to be disciples." Ambrose's style of hymn-singing soon spread throughout the west. It is certainly one of his greatest and most living legacies to us.

Of Ambrose's influence on imperial policy something has already been said in connexion with the statue of Victory controversy.[2] Two others must be quoted, the one favourably the other with distaste, because each was to help to form a pattern for future ages. In the year 390 the people of Thessalonica had been stung to fury by the billeting on them of barbarian troops. Only some "incident" was needed to produce an open outbreak. This was provided by the garrison

---

[1] *Sermon against Auxentius*, § 34. Ambrose was himself a hymn-writer of distinction, several of whose hymns are to be found in our hymnals in translations of varying merit.   [2] pp. 130-1.

commander, a man called Botherich, who imprisoned a favourite charioteer for having committed a very indecent offence. The citizens, more interested in racing than in morals, demanded his release, and when that was denied them they murdered Botherich with disgusting savagery. Theodosius flew into an uncontrollable rage, and Ambrose's pleas for mercy, though often renewed, were of no avail: the court clique, jealous of the bishop's dominance, persuaded Theodosius to impose an "exemplary" punishment on the people of Thessalonica, that is to say to have them massacred. The order cancelling this brutal command arrived too late to save the citizens. At least 7,000 were killed in the crowded circus. Ambrose left Milan, and refused to meet Theodosius. Instead, he wrote him a letter in his own hand, in which he acknowledged the emperor's zeal and love for God, but insisted that for such a wicked crime an act of contrition was essential: as David had listened to Nathan, so let Theodosius harken to God's minister. He did. His anger passed, to be succeeded by remorse, remorse by penitence. Theodosius, surrounded by his court and subjects, stripped of his purple, knelt in humility to seek divine pardon. In the words of the late Professor Baynes: "Bishop and Emperor had proved each worthy of the other."[1]

The second instance in which Ambrose's influence proved paramount is sad to relate. Some Christian monks at Callinicum (Er-Rakka in Mesopotamia) had destroyed a Jewish synagogue. They had thus not only committed a sin but a crime as well, because the inviolability of Jewish synagogues was prescribed by law.[2] When the case was laid before Theodosius he at once ordered that the synagogue should be rebuilt at the expense of the Christian community. When Ambrose heard of this decision he protested with such vigour that in the end Theodosius yielded. He may have been precipitate in ordering that the fault of a few should be made good by the many; but that in principle Theodosius was right and Ambrose wrong there can be no question.

Ambrose was great, beyond dispute. His influence on Church practice was to be profound. He had a sympathy with the subordinate and enslaved which was unusual in his day. He did not hesitate to turn church plate into cash to help the needy and oppressed. He asserted the right of the Church to guide princes in spiritual affairs. He established the right of the laity

---

[1] *Cambridge Medieval History*, Vol. I, p. 245.
[2] See p. 115, note 1 above.

to participate fully in the conduct of divine service. Ambrose was no great theologian; and yet it was by his preaching that he achieved the greatest single triumph of his life: the turning towards God of Augustine; but of that more must be said below.

The second of the great triad was a man of a completely different stamp. Jerome was born, c. 340, of Christian parents at Striden, now Stridova, near Aquileia, up in the "corner" of Italy, where the frontiers of Dalmatia and Pannonia met. At an early age he came to Rome, where he shewed himself to be a brilliant scholar. Like the rest of his contemporaries, he learned "rhetoric", but unlike many of them, Jerome captured the spirit of the classics as well as the letter. He moved in smart society, and led the life of a play-boy, for which he was later not only to feel himself but to inflict on others an exaggerated remorse. He travelled a good deal, and one of his journeys took him to Trier, at that time an imperial residence. It was here that he heard tell of the wonders of Egyptian monachism. The young scholar was deeply impressed. Here, perhaps, was to be found the cure for his follies and weaknesses? He would at least try. People in Rome had heard about this new way of life, but no one had tried it. Jerome would be a pioneer. In 373, when he was somewhat over thirty years of age, he collected a group of friends, said farewell to secular pleasures and set out for Syria. He travelled by way of Thrace, Athens and Asia Minor, and settled for a time at Antioch, at that period, as for so long before, the predominantly Hellenistic capital of the Roman province of Syria. As a retreat from carnal cares, Antioch was no better than Rome: Jerome must go farther. And so he went to live a life of rigid asceticism in the desert of Chalcis, near what is now Aleppo. It was a remarkable experience for a soft-bred young Roman. The other monks were mostly peasants. They talked Greek or Aramaic. It was easier for them to support the harsh life of the wilderness than it was for Jerome. He found he had little in common with them, and they seldom met except in church. But Jerome, who was not of a strong constitution, stuck it for more than five years.

It was while in his desert cell that he had the famous dream which he had recorded, no doubt embellished a little, in a letter to his pupil Eustochium.[1] He was rapt into the presence of God himself. "Such a dazzling light radiated from those who stood by, that, prostrate on the ground, I dared not

[1] *Letter* XXII.

raise my eyes. When I was asked what my profession was, I
said: 'I am a Christian'. 'You lie,' said He who presided,
'You are a Ciceronian, not a Christian: where your treasure
is, there shall your heart be also.' " Jerome swore that thence-
forth he would shun secular letters. Psychologically, the dream
is of the first interest, because it shews what the conflict was
that a Christian who was also a scholar had to face in the last
days of the struggle between the dying paganism and the new
Faith which was now come to maturity. Jerome was only the
most famous of many.

It was this outspoken frankness of Jerome, his inability to
hide his feelings, to hedge or to compromise, sometimes even
to shew good manners, that drove him into countless controversies and squabbles during his life; but it is also the quality
which endeared him to the men and women of the Middle
Ages and the Renaissance. It may seem odd to us that Jerome
was the subject of so many paintings: no saint has been represented more often. Sometimes he is shewn in the desert,
struggling with his spiritual enemies, sometimes in ecstasy,
sometimes in his study, sometimes even as a cardinal, and not
seldom with a lion for companion, a picturesque addition
dating from the sixth century. If we view sanctity in the guise
of a kind of beatified sweetness – as was the fashion during
a large part of the nineteenth century – then we must confess
that Jerome would not figure in the establishment; but the folk
of the Middle Ages and the epoch that succeeded them liked
their saints to be tough. And Jerome, the darling of Roman
drawing-rooms, the scintillating talker and scholar, who might
have been excused for being a smooth man, he it was who was
to prove himself as hardy as the sons of thunder, and to take
the kingdom of heaven, as it were, by storm.

A lesser man, having failed to adapt himself to the ascetic
life, would have kept away from Rome, where taunts and sneers
awaited him. Not so Jerome. After three fruitful years in
Constantinople, he returned to the capital in 382, summoned
by the pope, Damasus, who made him his secretary. Jerome's
enemies were furious. As soon as Damasus was dead – he died
in 384 – they made Rome too hot for Jerome: indeed, in 385
he had to leave the Eternal City without even saying goodbye
to his many friends. He simply collected his precious books,
dashed down to Ostia, and disappeared. He was bound for
the Holy Land. He knew now what his life-work was to be.
No longer would he consort with his rich ladies, however

godly, on the Aventine, no longer frequent the corridors of power. Pope Damasus had suggested to him that he revise the Latin text of the holy Scriptures; and he had already, in 383, published the Gospels, to be followed soon after by the remainder of the New Testament. No one was better fitted to undertake this task. While he was in Syria, Jerome had devoted himself to the study of the Bible. He had learned Greek and Latin as a boy, and to those two languages he had added Hebrew while in Syria, having found a converted Jew to instruct him, and Chaldean. He had been ordained priest almost against his will in Antioch in 379, but decided that he would not exercise his priestly functions, partly from a sense of inadequacy, partly because he wanted to be free to concentrate upon his biblical labours.

With him Jerome had brought his younger brother, Paulinianus, and two devout friends, Paula and her daughter Eustochium, "his daughters in Christ" as he called them. At Jerusalem, which they reached by way of Cyprus and Antioch, the proconsul offered the hospitality of his palace to pilgrims so eminent; but Paula insisted that, in the city where her Master had suffered, a more modest lodging must suffice. Besides, Jerusalem was not their goal. What Jerome sought was solitude. Jerusalem, he knew and said, was like any other provincial capital and garrison town, full of secular bustle and diversion, not all of it by any means sinless. The Mount of Olives was already occupied by recluses, who served the splendid foundations of the empress Helena. No, it was to Bethlehem that the little group must remove. Bethlehem was then, as it was to remain right up to the days, little more than a century ago, when Roberts and Lear sketched it, a small compact village clustered around the great basilica of the Nativity. It stands, as Jerusalem does, atop the ridge of the Judaean hills, nearly 3,000 feet above the Mediterranean to the west, and more than 4,000 above the leaden waters of the Dead Sea to the east, from which it is separated by the gaunt and lunar wilderness of Judaea, whereon ranged tribes of Bedu. They still do, but now they live in peace, and come to Bethlehem for the Saturday market to buy provisions and to sell their textiles and artifacts, and perhaps a fragment or two of a Scroll from the caves down at Qumran, above the Dead Sea; but in Jerome's day the Bedu were still as Ammianus had described them, "desirable neither as friends nor as enemies".[1] The only

[1] XIV, 4, 1.

other occupants of the desert were a few hermits. To add to the gloom of this austere scene, just where the sown gives way to the desert stood the brooding and sinister cone of Herod the Great's palace-tomb, a perpetual reminder of one who had brought bane to Bethlehem. The basilica of the Nativity itself was not the building we now behold, except for the mosaic floor which underlies the existing pavement, but the original shrine of Constantine, which was to be wholly reconstructed, the first materials being re-used, in the days of Justinian.

Such was the retreat that Jerome was to make the centre of his life and work. Before settling there the little cavalcade made a trip through southern Palestine, and visited Alexandria and the deserts of Egypt, where Christian monks had now replaced the children of Israel. In May of 386 they were back in Bethlehem and set about building two convents, one for the religious ladies assembled by Paula, the other for monks who wanted to live under the direction of Jerome, with a hostel for pilgrims, visitors or seekers after instruction. For it must be remembered that Jerome was already a famous authority. He had already, between 379 and 382, at Constantinople, translated thirty-seven homilies of Origen, the great Greek apologist of the third century. There he had studied with St Gregory of Nazianzus, who helped him to perfect his Greek, on his first journey to Syria, and from him had learned the method of allegorical interpretation of Scripture which he was to raise to such a pitch of virtuosity.

"In his double foundation," says Abel,[1] "Jerome sought to realize the ideal of cenobitic monachism: renunciation of family and the possession of worldly goods, the practice of poverty even in the furnishing of places of worship, abstention from wine and from all stimulating food, separation of the sexes, manual labour, assiduous Bible-reading both for the enrichment of the spirit and the conduct of life, chanting of the psalms, divided according to the six canonical hours, and on Sundays attendance at and participation in the sacred mysteries in the basilica of the Nativity. Apart from food and clothing, no sister might have anything of her own. . . . The sisters, even of the most noble origin, did not shrink from turning their hands to the humblest tasks of the kitchen and the sewing-room, not forgetting the making of clothes for the poor and needy of Bethlehem. The proximity of the Manger was a

[1] *Histoire de la Palestine depuis la conquête d'Alexandre jusqu'à l'invasion arabe,* II, p. 303.

constant sermon on humility. As Jerome wrote to Marcella: 'In the village of Christ all is rusticity; apart from the psalms all is silence.' "

This was not wholly true. Around the great star there formed almost at once a nebula of controversy. Jerome fell out with the bishop of Jerusalem. Epiphanius, bishop of Salamis in Cyprus, with whom Jerome had stayed on his way to the Levant, came to Palestine uninvited, bent on a heresy hunt: he was convinced that the great Origen had really been of unorthodox opinions. Jerome sided with the intruding prelate against his own metropolitan: the conventuals of the Mount of Olives were drawn in. Finally, things became so serious that the government actually issued a decree of banishment against Jerome, who was rescued from exile only by the death of the minister Rufinus,[1] who had signed the warrant. Another fracas was provoked by a group of heretics called Pelagians, after a British monk called Pelagius (né, most probably, Morgan), who denied the necessity of grace, free-will being in his, proleptically British, view sufficient to secure a man's salvation: he has only to will that he be virtuous, and virtuous he will be. Pelagius himself became the epicentre of a disturbance that swept Africa and Palestine no less than Rome, and it was some time before his heretical views met with definitive condemnation. Before that, both Augustine and Jerome had been involved. In the year 416 a band of Pelagian monks attacked and burned Jerome's convents, the inhabitants of which were forced to take refuge in the towers built to defend them against the Bedu; but the next year Pelagius was expelled from the country.

Pelagius, Epiphanius, even Origen – but few remember them now, and they have been cited only to shew that Jerome's retreat in the Holy Land was by no means a haven of uninterrupted peace. But of all his controversies the saddest was his dispute with St Augustine. It arose simply from a most deferential enquiry by Augustine concerning what he took to be an unorthodox commentary by Jerome on a passage in Galatians regarding the difference of opinion between Paul and Peter.[2] By a chain of mishaps, this letter, written in 394, was only delivered nine years after it had been despatched from Hippo.[3] Three years later, in 397, Augustine wrote a second letter to Jerome,[4] which, long before it reached Beth-

[1] See p. 53 above.   [2] *Galatians*, II, 11–14.   [3] *Letter* XXVIII.
[4] *Letter* XL.

lehem, had been circulated without Augustine's knowledge. When it was finally delivered into Jerome's hands it aroused his indignation, because it repeated the criticism Augustine had formerly made. Finally, in 402, Augustine wrote a third letter[1] which not only won over Jerome to Augustine's view but won Jerome's tough old heart as well.

Meanwhile the great work had been accomplished. The Bible stood complete in its new and scholarly Latin version. Jerome had added the Old Testament to the New. It had been a mountainous labour. In antiquity an accurate text of any work was hard to come by. The best copyists make mistakes, through lack of understanding, carelessness, weariness, monotony or inability to read their predecessors' script. Jerome himself suffered from faulty transmission. To give but one example, in the letter to Eustochium already quoted he refers to David's sin with Bathsheba. The scribe who copied the letter for publication knew his topography better than his Bible, and put "Beersheba", the town in southern Palestine, in place of "Bathsheba"; and nearly all our manuscripts have perpetuated the blunder. In a school, before a class on, say, Virgil, could begin, the master had to see that all the copies of his pupils agreed, or have them corrected to accord with what he thought the best text. In Jerome's day there existed various Latin versions of the Bible but, as Pope Damasus had realized, they differed widely. Jerome used the existing translations, but he went back to the original Greek for the New Testament, and for the Old to the Greek version known as the Septuagint and to the earlier Hebrew originals. He edited the whole corpus of the Scriptures, employing the diacritical marks, the asterisk and the obelus, which the Alexandrines had brought into vogue in dealing with classical texts. Jerome had spent fifteen years in checking his sources. These, it may be noted, were far more trustworthy, more "pure" than those of any classical writer. The Jews were meticulous in their literary transmission, as in everything else that touched their faith. The Christians were very soon able to circulate excellent copies of their own scriptures. Constantine had ordered bishop Eusebius of Caesarea to prepare a number of complete Bibles on parchment, the first books of their kind, of which the Codex Sinaiticus now in the British Museum may have been one. Earlier copies of the Gospels are known, written on papyrus. The earliest of these in book form contains the gospels of

[1] *Letter* LXVII.

L

St Luke and St John. It dates from the second century, and is now in the Bodmer library in Geneva. No classical manuscript can come within centuries of such a close link with the originals.

Jerome's great work, known as the Vulgate, is still the official Bible of the Roman Catholic Church. It is marked by vigour, aptness of expression and a flair amounting to genius for catching the meaning rather than the letter of the original. "At the very period when Latin was becoming the liturgical language of the West, when the division between the two halves of the Christian world was drawing near, Jerome gave the Latin Church scriptural bases so solid that sixteen centuries have not destroyed them."[1]

Jerome died in the year 420. He left behind him this great monument. He left, too, much exegetical and polemical literature (which few now read) and over a hundred letters. It is these letters that give us the real Jerome, tough, splenetic, headstrong, sometimes laughable, but nearly always lovable. There he sat, in his simple cell, hard at work. A horseman clatters up the hill. The letter is brought in. Jerome reads it; at once, on the spur of the moment he calls for a stenographer and dictates a reply. Back spurs the waiting messenger with the precious rescript, to gladden and inform a correspondent in Italy, Africa or Spain. From all over the Latin world came requests for enlightenment and advice. Jerome may claim to have founded the first correspondence college.

We have no portrait of Jerome, as we have of St Ambrose. But Augustine, who never met him, writes in his letter of 394 that he feels he knows him well, and what he looks like, through what he has heard of him. As was said above, by those who like their saints soft, Jerome was for long neglected and misprised. To our own age the Boanerges of Bethlehem makes a direct appeal: if only because he did as much as anyone to ensure that the Roman spirit, in all its marmoreal individuality and in its own majestic tongue, should abide and continue to our own epoch.

[1] Daniel-Rops, *The Church of Apostles and Martyrs*, p. 546.

CHAPTER XII

AUGUSTINE THE CITIZEN AND SAINT

We have now reached the final stage of this modest enquiry, and have arrived at the man whose name has glittered, perhaps, like a golden thread from time to time in the drab web of the foregoing narrative – Augustine of Hippo.

Augustine is one of the universal men. He ranks with Leonardo, with Newton, with Einstein, as one of the very few human geniuses, and the first, at that, to set the feet of humanity on to a new path, to get them moving again, when they seemed to be stuck, to induce them, above all, to look forward and not back. Augustine, even if he had never existed except as a fictional character, would still command our devotion, like, let us say, Myishkin in *The Idiot*, on account of the life he led, the romance which it diffuses. Fortunately for us, the *Confessions* of Augustine, far from being fiction, are one of the truest, frankest and most heart-lifting autobiographies ever written. It is from them, above all, that we can construct for ourselves the tale of this remarkable life, which was to be the framework of an even more remarkable achievement; so that it is well to begin with them. Even so, the book cannot be classed as "background material", because it is dominated by two beings, Augustine and God.

Augustine was born on 13th November, 354, at a little Numidian town called Tagaste, to-day Sūq al-Ahras in Algeria. The town, now a busy railway depôt, lies in a beautiful setting. When we think of the "Africa" of Augustine we must banish any idea of either sand or swamps: northern Africa is the counterpart of southern Spain. The plains are broad and fertile, irrigated by the streams that flow down from the mountains on whose flanks flourish thick groves of oak and cork trees. It is a most green and pleasant land, specially in spring, and it was a fitting cradle, this little hill town set among the woods, for its greatest son. Augustine bore a Roman name, Aurelius Augustinus, but he was a son of Africa, of that mixture of Punic and Berber which had given Rome some of its most outstanding emperors. His father, Patricius, was a pagan, his mother, Monica, the daughter of a family which had been

Christian for several generations, and a saint if ever there was one. Thus from his very conception Augustine represented the problem, the assimilation of the old and the new, of which he was, above all other men, to provide the solution.

Augustine's recollections of his childhood are remarkably vivid; how, for instance, he gradually came to know the names of things, and to substitute words for grunts.¹ How many people ordinarily do remember so early a stage of development? As a schoolboy he was undisciplined and idle and, despite frequent beatings, often played truant.² And here at the outset of this *histoire d'une âme* we may note two characteristics which are peculiarly its author's. First, he regards any deviation from perfection as a sin, not as a mere flaw, human and inevitable; secondly, he is not in retrospect tormented by it. In this regard he is quite different from Jerome, who as an old man in Bethlehem was constantly haunted, as his letters shew, by remorse for the sins of his youth. When, with a frankness which shocked Dill,³ Jerome describes to Eustochium the carnal temptations to which a virgin is liable, with the distressing physical consequences which yielding to them entails, he is, we can see, colouring the lurid picture with his own personal reminiscences. He is a tortured extremist, for whom the best to be said of marriage is that it perpetuates the output of virgins. Augustine, on the other hand, is serene in writing of his former sins, because he is absolutely confident that all, small as well as great, have been forgiven, and have ceased to exist. So, after telling us what a bad boy he was at school, he adds this little prayer: "Look down upon these things mercifully, O Lord, and deliver us that now call upon thee: deliver also those that do not yet call upon thee; that they may call upon thee, and thou mayest deliver them."⁴ He was to regard his later lapses, such as orchard-robbing and keeping a mistress, in exactly the same light. This has puzzled, indeed disconcerted, readers brought up in a tradition which had more in common with Jerome's outlook; but it is essential to any understanding of Augustine's philosophy to grasp that for him there were only two alternatives, life and its absence: between them there could be no gradations, and consequently no compromise.

Tagaste held no future for a lad who was keen to shine, even if only in sports and pranks. His father Patricius, before he died, had noticed an improvement in his son. The boy now

---

¹ *Confessions*, I, viii.   ² *Ibid.*, I, ix.   ³ *op. cit.*, p. 127.
⁴ *Confessions*, I, x.

clearly had an aptitude for Latin, though Greek he "hated", without knowing why.[1] He never did master Greek. In his first letter to Jerome, already quoted, before he comes to the controversial part, he writes: "We beg you then (and we are joined in this by all the company of students in the African churches) not to refuse to devote toil and trouble to translating the works of those who have so excellently expounded our Scriptures in Greek." It was on Latin that Augustine, like Ambrose and Jerome, was to concentrate. First he went to the town of Madaura, some twenty miles from his home, and then on to Carthage, the great city on the sea-coast 120 miles to the east, the intellectual centre of the whole of Roman Africa. Carthage lay on the lovely bay that now shelters the city of Tunis. Not even the gulf of Naples offers a more caressing prospect, with the dim, hyacinthine mountains rising and receding above the azure waters. The city, the proud Punic capital, had been destroyed in 146 B.C.; but under the Antonines it had been gloriously reborn. Villas, baths, a theatre, an amphitheatre, a magnificent aqueduct, the gift of the emperor Hadrian, all the amenities of a Roman colonial centre were furnished in profusion. Also carnal temptations.

At the age of fifteen, Augustine tells us[2] with his accustomed frankness, "when that father of mine saw me in the bath, budding into manhood, and endued with a stirring adolescence, as though from this sight he first set his heart on having grandchildren by me, he told my mother about it, with much satisfaction (much bibulous satisfaction it was)". The reaction of the two parents was different: "Thou hadst already begun thy temple in my mother's heart, and laid the foundations of thy holy habitation, whereas my father was only a catechumen, and a recent one at that." But the outcome was the same from each parent. Looking back, Augustine wished that "the high tides of my youth had spent their foam upon the shore of marriage". Augustine was not yet baptized (he nearly had been, as a child, when he fell dangerously ill, but on his recovery, the rite, with its inherent obligations, had been deferred); his father therefore considered that a wife would merely be a hindrance to a rising young professor: his mother, sensible woman, saw little advantage in her son's entering upon a contract which she knew he was quite incapable of keeping. She also shared her husband's view, but for a different reason.

[1] *Ibid.*, I, xiii.
[2] *Ibid.*, II, iii.

Monica believed that it would be through his learned profession that her son would be brought to God.

Both parents were proved right. Augustine rounded off
his education, though in later life he was a critic of its methods:
the rules of grammar were regarded as being more important
than the laws of God, and barbarisms of speech more to be
blamed than corruption of manners. He can also look back
with the eye of a saint-psychologist on his emotional development. Love he had not yet known. "I was not yet in love, but
I did love to be in love, and with a more secret sort of want,
I hated myself for wanting so little."[1] In the place of love, he
substituted lust, competitive lust, even to the extent of boasting
of adventures he had not experienced. And to lust he added
sentiment, the feigned emotions provoked by the theatre.

It was at the age of nineteen that Augustine received his
first spiritual stimulus, when in the ordinary routine of his
studies he came upon the *Hortensius* of Cicero "whose tongue
almost everybody admires, his heart not so much... This book
quite altered my affection, turned my prayers to thyself, O
Lord, and made me have quite different aims and objects."
Monica had been right. Augustine now took up the Bible;
but he soon put it down again – the style was too crude for
one trained in the fashionable classics.[2] So instead of becoming
a Christian, he joined the sect of the Manichees, and stayed
with them as a simple auditor for nine whole years. Although
after his conversion Augustine wholly repudiated the doctrines
of the Manicheans, more than one reader of his works has
inclined to believe that the Manichean dualism, even when
rejected, nevertheless left a deep mark on Augustine's philosophy, with its constant antithesis of right and wrong, light and
darkness.

Meanwhile Augustine was back in his native town of
Tagaste, as a professor, and was living with the unnamed
woman of whom the *Confessions* tell us nothing. He tried
astrology, but soon gave it up: magic sacrifices, he is careful to
tell us, he never did dabble in.[3]

The death of a dear friend reduced him to such a state of
nervous exhaustion that he could no longer face the daily
round, and so he went again to Carthage, where he had been
offered a post as teacher of rhetoric. He remained there about

---

[1] *Ibid.*, III, i. The contrived "conceit" in which this revelation is phrased
is typical of the style which Augustine had been taught to imitate.

[2] *Ibid.*, III, iv and v.   [3] *Ibid.*, IV. ii.

eight years, but finally became disgusted at the indiscipline of his unruly pupils. He decided to try his fortune in Rome, where things would be better ordered. His mother was against the plan; but Augustine gave her the slip. Saying that he was going to see a friend off at the harbour, he bade Monica go and pray in the oratory of St Cyprian, the bishop of Carthage who had suffered martyrdom there in the year 258. By the time his mother came back, Augustine was on board a ship bound for Italy.

He was now twenty-nine. He had ceased to be a Manichee, he was not yet a Christian. He had sampled Aristotle, and relished him.[1] He now turned towards the theorists of the New Academy, who maintained that a wise man would content himself with probability, absolute truth being unattainable. Rome, too, proved a disappointment: the pupils might be better behaved, but they were less honest. They would attend a course by one professor, and then, when it came to paying their fees, they simply made off, and joined the classes of another.

But the great climax of Augustine's life was at hand. The city of Milan was advertising for a master of rhetoric. Augustine entered the competition, delivered a public oration and was declared the winner. By whom? By none other than our old friend Symmachus, the illustrious pagan, and prefect of the city. It was he, no less, who was to despatch Augustine on the journey which was to lead to his conversion. Symmachus the saint-maker: it is one of history's most satisfactory jokes.

"And so," says Augustine,[2] "I came to Milan, to bishop Ambrose, a man of the highest reputation everywhere, and a faithful servant of Thine... To him was I led by Thee unknowing, so that knowing I might be led to Thee by him. That man of God took me up like a father, and like the good bishop he was, approved my peregrination. So I began to love him, not to start with as a teacher of the truth, because I never dreamed of finding that in the Church, but simply because he was so kind to me. I used to go regularly to hear him preach in public, with no particular object in mind, as I should have had, but to test his eloquence, whether it was all it was made out to be, or greater or less than people said. I hung on his words[3]

---

[1] *Ibid.*, IV, xvi. He had read the *Categories*, probably in translation. It is the only work of Aristotle which we know for certain that he did read.

[2] *Ibid.*, V, xiii. Note again the tiresome affectation of phrase. Only an Augustine could make it seem irrelevant, so true is his meaning.

[3] "*Verbis eius suspendebar intentus.*"

intently, but I was contemptuously careless of the subject-matter. I was delighted with the charm of his discourse: it was more learned than that of Faustus [his Manichean tutor], though not so exciting and seductive – I mean the style of delivery: when it came to the substance, there was no comparison. Faustus wandered about in his Manichean fallacies, whereas Ambrose taught salvation, most soundly. Salvation is a long way off from sinners, such as I was then. But I was getting nearer to it, gradually and without knowing it."

Thus does one saint describe his attraction to God by another.

The crisis came in July, 386, when Augustine was thirty-two. He had been studying the Bible and also the Neo-Platonists, by whom he was powerfully attracted, as so many devout Christians would be after him. His mother had now joined him, and seeing how his spiritual life was developing, urged him to put away his concubine. He did, and then took another: he was still the "liméd soul that struggling to be free, art more engaged".[1]

His final liberation, the transformation from rip to saint, is one of the most famous conversions in history. It ranks with that of Paul of Tarsus. Like that experience, we have record of it (how could it be otherwise?) only from the recipient himself. Of Paul's we have four versions, of Augustine's one only; but the same basic criterion applies to both cases. It is quite beside the point, when discussing religious experience, be it conversion, miracle or vision, to adopt an exterior view: what we think the experience might have been, could not have been or should according to our enlightened ideas have been are all equally irrelevant. The one and only point of any significance or consequence is what the recipient felt and recalled himself as having felt, expressed in terms of his own cognizance. Here is Augustine's own account[2] (he had been discussing his state of mind and soul with his great friend Alypius, who shared his home in Milan. Augustine, overcome

---

[1] Augustine's views on sexual love were at this period those of his age. It must be remembered that concubinage was regarded as a natural safeguard against its unnatural and only too prevalent alternative, pederasty. Lecky's classic apology for "the eternal priestess of humanity, blasted for the sins of the people" in Chapter XIV of his *History of European Morals* may be applied to the world of Rome as aptly as to that of Greece.

Augustine was no cold Puritan. He extols the beauty of the human body both on the *Confessions* (II, v) and in the *City of God* (XXII, 24). When it came to sex, Augustine was never one to beat about the bush.

[2] *Ibid.*, VIII, xii.

with tears, got up and left him, much to Alypius' astonishment):
"I flung myself down under a fig-tree, I cannot remember
how, and gave full rein to my tears. The floods of my eyes
gushed out, an acceptable sacrifice to Thee, O Lord. I then
said – not in these exact words, but in this sense – 'And Thou,
O Lord, how long, how long wilt thou be angry: for ever?
Remember not our former offences';[1] because I found myself
still holden by them. I cried out in my wretchedness, 'How
long, how long? To-morrow and to-morrow? Why not
now? Why not this very hour put an end to my depravity?'
I was talking like this, and crying, in the most bitter contrition
of heart. Then suddenly I hear a voice from the house next
door, of a boy or girl, I don't know which, singing: 'take up
and read, take up and read'. At once I changed my looks,
and started to think furiously: did children ever use these
words in any game? I could not remember that they ever
did. I stopped my violent weeping and got up, interpreting
it as nothing else but a divine command that I should open the
Book and read the first verse I found. (I had heard that
Antony [the hermit] by hearing the Gospel that he once
chanced to come in at, took it as a personal admonition, as
if what was being read were addressed to him: Go, and sell
that thou hast and give to the poor, and thou shalt have treasure
in heaven, and come and follow me; and that it was by such
a miracle he was at once converted to Thee.) So I at once went
back to where Alypius was sitting, because I had put the
apostle's book down there when I got up. I snatched it, opened
it, and in silence read the first passage which met my eyes:
'Not in rioting and drunkenness, not in chambering and wan-
tonness, not in strife and envying: but put ye on the Lord
Jesus Christ; and make no provision for the flesh to fulfil the
lusts thereof.'[2] I did not want to read any farther, not did I
need to. For instantly, as I reached the end of the sentence,
by a light of confidence as it were poured into my heart, all
the darkness of doubt was dispelled."

Nine months after his conversion, on 24th April, 387,
Augustine received baptism at the hands of Ambrose, together
with Alypius, and his son by his concubine, Adeodatus (God-
given). Before the ceremony he had sent the bishop a plenary
confession, together with an undertaking to renounce his sins
for ever. A friend lent him a country house at Cassiciacum
(Cassago di Brianza, some twenty miles north of Milan, in

---

[1] *Psalms*, VI, 3, and LXXIX, 5.   [2] *Romans*, XIII, 13-14.

the foothills of the Alps), where he spent a short retreat. Then, having resigned his professorship – as from the end of the academic year, so as not to cause unpleasant comment – he set out once again for Africa. Monica, full of joy, was with him. At Ostia, their port of embarkation for Africa, Monica fell ill, and died. She was fifty-five, he thirty-two. Augustine gives us a beautiful and grateful obituary notice of her. It contains the sentence: "neither did she die unhappy, nor did she die altogether".[1]

Augustine landed at Carthage, the port he had left four years earlier, as a very different man. He went back to Tagaste, but only to sell what property his father had left him, give the proceeds to the poor and then to establish himself and a few companions in what must be accounted the first Augustinian society. He was already, by reason of his personality, reputation and literary activity, famous throughout North Africa. All he wanted was to live the cloistered religious life, "to be a monk not a minister. He felt the need to organize his community in a more regular fashion, in a new locality with an established rule. But that was all; and in order to avoid being consecrated against his will, he carefully avoided churches which he knew, at any time, to be without a bishop".[2]

But in the year 391 Augustine visited Hippo Regius, a seaport some fifty miles distant from Tagaste, later to be known as Bône, and now called 'Annāba. Until recently, but little of the ancient city had been uncovered, because it was believed that it had been completely destroyed by the Vandals. The excavations of the last twenty years, however, have brought to light extensive remains of a flourishing Roman city, with basilicas, villas, shops, splendid baths, modelled on those of Caracalla in Rome, and the largest forum in the whole of Roman Africa, constructed entirely of marble. This splendid city, which had prospered even in Phoenician times, is set in a horseshoe of mountains, and fronts the waters of the Mediterranean. Because, on the southern shore of the Mediterranean as he faces the sea, the sun is generally behind the spectator,

---

[1] "*Nec misere moriebatur nec omnino moriebatur.*" A recollection perhaps of Horace's "*Non omnis moriar*". Monica is commemorated to-day by a plaque bearing this phrase amid the ruins of Ostia.

[2] *St Augustine of Hippo: Life and Controversies*, by Gerald Bonner, p. 111. This excellent book is strongly recommended to those who wish to make a study of St Augustine; as is Henri-Irénée Marrou's *Saint Augustin et la Fin de la Culture Antique*. I gratefully acknowledge my indebtedness to both of them.

and not shining in his eyes, this coast gives the impression of being "the fourth wall" of the theatre of civilization, and the feeling of the drama of mankind is thereby notably heightened. This is strikingly true of Hippo Regius. Augustine went there to see a friend in the secret police who he thought might adopt the monastic life. In the course of his visit he attended service in the great church, of which the floor and lower courses still survive. Augustine felt safe, because Hippo had a bishop; but that very day Bishop Valerius, who was old and, being a Greek, found preaching to a Latin- and Punic-speaking congregation a strain, said in his sermon that he really must have a priest to help him.

It was Ambrose all over again, almost. The congregation, which had recognized Augustine, seized hold of him and dragged him up to the bishop for ordination, despite his tearful protests. So Augustine became priest of Hippo.

The bishop gave him a garden near the cathedral, wherein to build a monastery. "He was joined by his friends from Tagaste, including Alypius, Evodius and Severus, while new recruits subsequently came forward: Possidius, the future bishop of Calama and Augustine's biographer; Profuturus, afterwards bishop of Cirta; Urban, the future bishop of Sicca; and Peregrinus, who was to preside over the church of Thenae. It is possible that a written rule was provided, though we have no proof of this."[1]

So successful was the new priest, both as a preacher and as an author, that he was consecrated bishop co-adjutor in 395; the following year, at the age of forty-two, on the death of Valerius, he became bishop of Hippo, the see he was to administer for more than thirty years. He died in the year 430, on 28th August, with the Vandals hammering on the doors of the city, which they were to enter eleven months later. Augustine died in full possession of sight, hearing and all his faculties, with the seven penitential psalms written on vellum hung up before his eyes.[2] He was in his seventy-sixth year.

The literary activity of Augustine was sustained and prolific. Despite his poor health, his insomnia and bronchitis, he was a most energetic pastor. Much of his talent was deployed in the refutation of heresy, to confounding the Donatists, the Manichees, the Pelagians. He wrote, too, an astounding number of theological treatises, and innumerable letters, of which numbers survive, and preached sermon after sermon.

[1] Bonner, *op. cit.*, p. 114.   [2] *Ibid.*, p. 155.

But, for the ordinary man, and it is the ordinary men and women who make up the world, the fame and influence of Augustine rest upon two works, the *Confessions* and the *City of God*. The former work, written shortly after his consecration as bishop, has already been quoted. The newly made bishop wanted to make it quite clear how he had reached the stage in his spiritual pilgrimage he had now attained. We live in an age of outspoken prelates; but it is hard to imagine that any of them would be quite so frank about his former life. In fact the personal, autobiographical aspect of the *Confessions* is dimmed, for all its prismatic brilliance, by the incandescent light of Augustine's faith, his poetic but always controlled ecstasy, above all, by his steadfast aim, which is to shew forth not the failings of a sinner, but the overmastering grace of that sinner's God. There is nothing in the whole range of ancient literature to be set beside the *Confessions;* but that is because the book does not belong to ancient literature: it is the first "modern" autobiography. Here we have, beyond question, the old Roman idiom, even down to its idiosyncrasies, as noted above, used as the vehicle for a new, universal, analysis of personality. The supposedly eternal ice-caps of immemorial convention have melted before the rays of the newly risen, unclouded Sun, and have been transmuted into busy streams, whose office is to fertilize and to refresh.

The *City of God* is one of those works which have never been out of fashion or favour ever since they were written. The libraries of Europe contain more than 500 manuscripts of it: as soon as printing was invented, between 1467 and 1495 twenty-four editions of it appeared. It has been translated, edited, reprinted again and again. It is one of the living, germinal productions of the mind of man. In what does its power reside? Its chief claim to immortality is that it is the first really great essay in the philosophy of history. It was occasioned by Alaric's capture of Rome. That event had been hailed as a disaster, as the end of a world, of the world. Augustine himself had bewailed it, though not with the extravagant rhetoric of Jerome. But for Augustine, mere lamentation was not enough. For the man who throughout his life had insisted on "Truth, truth,"[1] who had refused to compromise with heresy, who had even remonstrated with Jerome when he knew that he was right, for such a man no mere disaster could be an end. And so he set out to demonstrate that the true

[1] *Confessions*, III, vi.

polity of God could not be contained within three dimensions. The whole work, which consists of twenty-two books, occupied such time as Augustine could spare from his duties for thirteen years (413–426). It falls into two distinct parts. The first, Books I to X, is critical. The standard scapegoat for the downfall of Rome was Christianity: the argument was too easy, not to say facile. Rome had done very well for a thousand years, until Christianity began to prevail; when it did, Rome fell. Augustine refutes this argument, with enormous erudition and a good deal of wit. To start with, he says, Rome had not done all that well; she had known many disasters, both from without, and from within during the civil wars. The gods had done nothing to stop these.[1] It was inconsistent of the pagans to impute a temporary disaster to the Christians, without saddling their own gods with the destruction of the republic, which as Cicero had pointed out, had ceased to exist in his day.[2] Sallust, "whom we learned at school for a fee", he, too, had blamed Rome for her "lust of domination": "the City had degenerated from being the most beautiful and best to the worst and most vicious".[3] The last time there had been an invasion from the north "the geese were awake, while the gods slept".[4] These inefficient gods seem to have proliferated without rhyme or reason. There were godlets for every conceivable thing and occasion, one god for the threshold, one for the hinge, a third for the door, whereas a single porter, being *human*, was enough.[5] Why not have a temple of Discord, which seemed more popular than Concord; why not, in a state which has waxed great on war, worship External Aggression?[6] Quiet, Augustine notes, was worshipped only outside the City[7] – a location which to many modern Romans would seem appropriate.

No, these gods have done nothing to help Rome; they are in reality mere demons. What made Rome great was not Rome's gods but its citizens. It was they who through love of praise raised Rome to her zenith. Love of praise may be a vice, but yet it can be a virtue, too, in so far as it checks other and worse vices.[8] In terms of *Matthew* VI, 2, the Romans have received their reward.

A more serious objection to these pagan god-demons is that

---

[1] *City of God*, III, xvi; xxix.
[2] *Ibid.*, II, xxv; xxi.
[3] *Ibid.*, II, xviii.
[4] *Ibid.*, II, xxii.
[5] *Ibid.*, IV, 8.
[6] *Ibid.*, IV, xv.
[7] *Ibid* IV, xvi.
[8] *Ibid.*, V. xii.

they cannot bestow eternal life.[1] (Augustine was by no means the first to say this: it had been a religious commonplace for centuries in Rome that those who sought *salus*, health of spirit, salvation, must seek it in the imported mystery religions, from Isis, from Sarapis or from Mithras.)

Such is the scope of the first, or critical, part of Augustine's thesis.

With the eleventh book, the argument becomes more elevated, more universal. We are no longer concerned with a local, topical dialectic. These attacks against Christianity, this hatred which the pagans are once again letting loose against the faithful – all this is simply one more episode in the eternal combat between the Heavenly City and the Earthly City, between the city where reigns the love of God to the despite of self, and the other where reigns the love of self to the despite of God.[2] These terms would be familiar to Augustine's readers, either from Platonic originals in the *Republic* or *Theaetetus*, or from the Bible itself. At the beginning of Book XI, Augustine refers specifically to Psalm LXXXVII, 3: "Glorious things are spoken of thee, O city of God." The idea of mankind divided into two categories is familiar also in the New Testament, e.g. in the *Epistle to the Hebrews*, or that of St Paul to the Romans. Ambrose, too, would use phrases such as *civitas Dei, regnum peccati* to denote believers and unbelievers.[3]

So Augustine defines the categories again. "We divide this human race," he writes,[4] "into two kinds, the one composed of men who live according to man, the other of those who live according to God: and we give them the mystical name of cities." In this very strict, indeed rigid, opposition of the two societies it is permissible to see a vestige of Augustine's discarded Manicheism. Carried to its logical conclusion, this antithesis would make the Roman empire the enemy of God; but Augustine is at pains not to say this. He was a loyal son of the state, proud of its culture, of which he himself was so bright an ornament. The state certainly possesses a certain civil authority. Even bad states must be obeyed.[5] Augustine is not a political theorist, but a moral philosopher bent on charting the course for humanity by moral and religious considerations. Yet he by no means neglects secular affairs, and the mundane setting in which mankind must perforce live – he was always a

---

[1] *Ibid.*, VI, i.   [2] *Ibid.*, XIV, xxviii.
[3] See Pierre de Labriolle, *Histoire de L'Eglise*, Vol. iv, p. 54 *et seq.*
[4] *City of God*, XV, 1.   [5] *Ibid.*, II, xix.

practical saint. War he regards as legitimate in self-defence, but conquest based on might is for him the *grande latrocinium*, "wholesale brigandage".[1] The ideal state is one in which Christian principles prevail, and can count on the support of the secular power; and yet the City of God is a pilgrim. Eventually it will achieve its goal: "The end of this City, in which it will have its highest good, is to be defined as either peace in eternal life, or eternal life in peace."[2] Does not this take us back, in the civic or national sphere, to the famous definition of personal destiny which occurs in the very first paragraph of the *Confessions*, "Unto thyself Thou hast made us, O Lord, and our heart is restless until it find rest in Thee"?

Societies may come and go, but above all these terrestrial and transient polities there stands the one indestructible polity, the true Eternal City, the City of God.

[1] *Ibid.*, IV, vi.

[2] *Ibid.*, XIX, li: "*Finis civitatis huius in quo summum habebit bonum, vel pax in vita eterna vel vita eterna in pace dicendus est.*"

CONCLUSION

With Augustine, we are already on the threshold of the Middle Ages. What then is the upshot of this modest enquiry?

1. That the Rome of the emperors and legions had perished is not to be denied. It had decayed within before it was overthrown from without. Rome was old, and no longer knew how to live. The resistance of the body politic was lowered, so that it fell a victim to internal and external assaults it no longer had the vitality to resist. To no one single cause can the eclipse be ascribed: it was the result of a general debility.

2. If no one factor can be isolated as having caused the end of Roman Rome, neither to the end itself can any one date be assigned. *Romanitas* survived Rome. From the north came new and vigorous men, intent on finding a home and founding a state in Italy. These men consciously fostered a Roman continuity. Indeed, as has been noted, it is a telling fact that the only two of the invading races who deliberately tried to eradicate Roman polity and tradition, namely the Huns and the Vandals, are the only two who were to have no part whatever in the making of the new Europe. They simply disappeared. If the Angles, Saxons and Jutes survived, it is nevertheless true that they did so only after two deliberate and massive attempts to re-civilize them, first in the sixth century by Pope Gregory and secondly in the eleventh by William the Norman.

3. The decay of the secular fabric was accompanied by the rise of the Church as the central repository of life and discipline, of the arts and of philosophy. The two events were contemporary; but it would be false to ascribe the former to the latter. On the contrary, it was the decline of the secular power that made men turn more and more to the Church for guidance and protection.

4. Both the successor states and the Church considered themselves, and justly, to be the heirs of imperial Rome. Each strove to be as Roman as possible. In that sense, therefore, the Roman world was transmitted, in its laws, its customs and its methods, to succeeding ages. It has not so far come to an end; nor, so long as states are organized on traditional "western"

lines whether monarchical or republican, is there any reason why it should.

The question inevitably arises: what parallel is there between the twentieth century, which has witnessed the dissolution of so many empires, and the fifth? The answer is, no very close one. Some of the symptoms of decay, such as defeated Rome, are, it is true, present in our own society. Crippling taxation, a civil service which has proliferated beyond the bounds of human relationship or public economy, and a general decline in the standards of conduct born of what Hodgkin (nearly a century ago) called "crowned socialism" – all these we share with the late Roman empire. But whereas the Roman state, as distinct from the Church, had no new resources with which to combat new evils, the twentieth century has. The possibilities of scientific achievement widen every year: man becomes more and more master of his world. To speak of this as simply "material" progress is to commit a great error: science in our day is to be reckoned among the arts, and as such part of man's spiritual pilgrimage. In this respect we can claim to be the superiors of the ancients.

So we can, on another plane, the most important and the most hopeful of all. Nowadays we all admit that we are our brothers' keepers. The relief of hunger and suffering, the succouring of the afflicted and distressed, the indivisibility of mankind, in fact, this is an axiom which in our own day has won the widest acceptance. It is as old as the Christian faith itself, whose founder taught it by precept and by example, as old, indeed, as Cain. It was quite unknown in antiquity. It is a paradox of the age that while the formulae of religious belief are increasingly challenged and discarded, the responsibilities of the Judaeo-Christian ethic are more widely and more willingly shouldered than ever before.

The fifth century was an age of despair: the twentieth may well be one of over-confidence. The cure for both those conditions is faith. And the practical manifestations of faith of this century, in its international co-operative efforts, and in the union of ordinary men and women, across the barriers of race and faith, for the welfare of their fellows, cannot be written down as mere "humanitarianism". We seem to be getting back, in logic and in practice, to the practical, logical belief of men like Ambrose, Jerome and Augustine, "for he that loveth not his brother whom he hath seen, how can he love God whom he hath not seen?"

M

There are greater institutions than empires. When they dissolve, those that dwell in them combine in new associations, both national and international, material and spiritual, but men remain what they have always been, and always will be, potential citizens of the true, Augustinian, Eternal City.

EMPERORS [1] AND POPES MENTIONED IN THE TEXT

n.d. = non-dynastic

* = Emperors in the East who later became sole emperor.

		Popes (All rank as saints)
Constantinian Dynasty A.D. 324–363		
Founder of dynasty Constantius I, 305–306		314–335 Sylvester
Constantine I 306, sole emperor 324–337		336–336 Marcus

West	*East*	
Constantine II 337–340	*Constantius II 337	337–352 Julius
Constans 337–350		

Sole Emperor		
*Constantius II 350–361		
Julian 361–363		352–366 Liberius
Jovian 363–364 (n.d.)		

Valentinean Dynasty A.D. 364–392

West	*East*	
Valentinian I 364–375	Valens 365–378	366–384 Damasus
Gratian 367–383	*Theodosius I 379–392 (n.d.)	
Valentinian II 375–392		384–398 Siricius

Theodosian Dynasty A.D. 392–457

Sole Emperor

*Theodosius I 392–395

West	*East*	
Honorius 395–423	Arcadius 395–408	398–401 Anastasius I
Constantius III 422	Theodosius II 408–450	402–417 Innocentius
Valentinian III 425–455	Marcian 450–457	417–418 Zosimus
Maximus 455 (n.d.)		418–422 Bonifacius
		422–433 Celestinus
Avitus 455–456 (n.d.)		433–440 Sixtus III
		440–461 Leo I

[1] For genealogies see Appendix II.

Leonine Dynasty A.D. 457–518

	West		East	
(all n.d.)				
Majorian	457–461	*Leo I	457–474	461–468 Hilarius
Severus	461–465			

Sole Emperor

	*Leo I	465–467		
Anthemius	467–472			468–483 Simplicius
Olybrius	472	Leo II	474	
Glycerius	473–474	Zeno	474–491	483–492 Felix III
Julius Nepos	474–480[1]	Anastasius I	491–518	492–496 Gelasius II
Romulus				496–498 Anastasius
Augustulus	475–476			498–514 Symmachus

Justinianean Dynasty

Justin I	518–527	514–523 Hormisdas
Justinian	527–565	523–526 Johannes I
	etc.	

[1] See note on page 88.

SOME GENEALOGIES

THE FAMILY OF CONSTANTINE

Crispus, brother of emperors Claudius II and Quintilius
|
Claudia, *m* Eutropius
|
Constantius Chlorus, Augustus in A.D. 305; *d* York A.D. 306; *m* 1. Helena the Saint, 2. Theodora

(by 1.)

CONSTANTINUS MAGNUS, *m* 1. Minervina; 2. Fausta, daughter of emperor Galerius and his second wife Eutropia

1.	2.	3.	4.	5.
Crispus; Caesar, 316; put to death by order of his father, 326; *m* Helena; issue unknown	Constantinus II, surnamed the Younger; *b* 312; Caesar, 316; Emperor, 377; *d* 340. Twice married (?); no issue known	Constantius II, *b* 317; Caesar, 326 (?); Emperor, 337; sole Emp., 353; *d* 361; *m* 1. unknown; 2. Flavia Aurelia Maxima Faustina	Constans; *b* 320; Caesar 333 (335?) Emp., 337; killed, 350; *m* Olympia; no issue known	Constantina or Constantia; *m* 1. her kinsman Hannibalianus, king of Pontus; 2. Constantine Gallus, emp.

For column 5, continued:
6. Constantia or Constantina; nun
7. Helena, Flavia Maximiana; *m* emperor Julian, her kinsman

|
Flavia Maxima Constantia, *m* emperor Gratian

(by 2.)

1.	2.	3.
Constantinus, murdered by emperor Constantius II; no issue known	Dalmatius Flavius Hannibalianus; time of death unknown	Constantius, Consul, 335; murdered by emperor Constantius; *m* 1. Galla; 2. Basilina

1.	2.
Dalmatius, Flavius Julius, Consul in A.D. 333. Put to death by emperor Constantine the Younger in 339 or 340; no issue known	Hannibalianus, Flavius Claudius, king of Pontus; *m* Constantina, eldest daughter of Constantine the Great; perished in the wholesale murder of his kinsmen

1.	2.	3.	4.
A son, killed by the emperor Constantius II in 341	Gallus, Flavius Julius, *b* 325; Caesar, 351; disobedient; put to death by emperor Constantius II near Pola, in Istria, 354; *m* Constantina, widow of Hannibalianus and eldest daughter of Constantine the Great	A daughter *m* emperor Constantius	Julianus, surnamed the Apostate; *b* 332(?); Caesar 355; succeeded Constantius in 361; killed in Persian War, 26th June, 363. *m* Helena, Flavia Maximiana, youngest daughter of Constantine the Great; left issue whose fate is unknown

4.	5.	6.
Constantia or Costantina Flavia Valeria, *m* in 313 Valeria Licinianus Licinius, Augustus; *d* between 328 and 330	Anastasia, *m* Bassianus Caesar, and after his death, probably, Lucius Ramius Aconitus Optatus, consul	Eutropia, *m* Popilius Nepotianus, consul
Flavius Licinianus Licinius, put to death by Constantine the Great	Flavius Popilius Nepotianus; assumed the purple in Gaul in 350; killed at Rome 350	

THE FAMILY OF VALENTINIAN
[Emperors of the east are printed in *Italic* capitals]

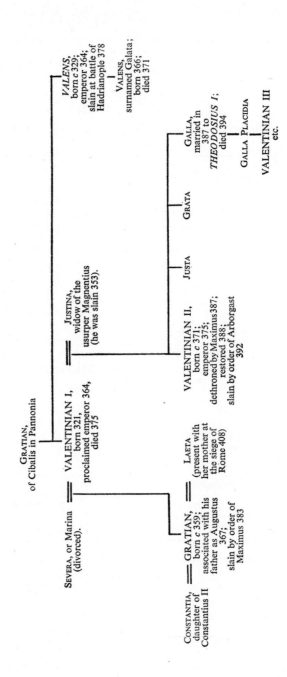

THE FAMILY OF THEODOSIUS
[Emperors of the east are printed in *italic* capitals]

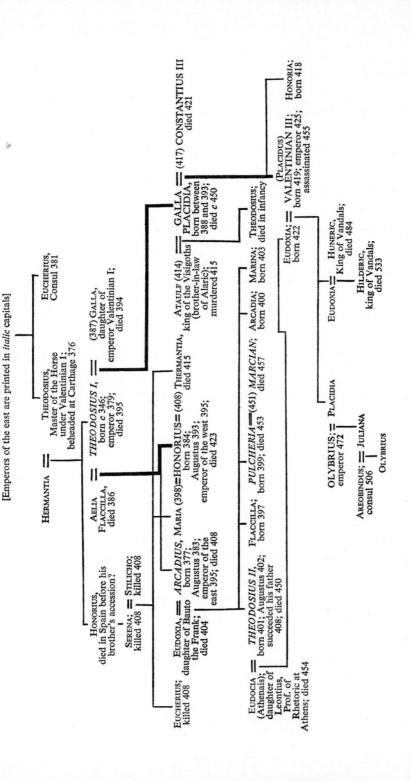

SOME DATES

(For emperors and popes see Appendix I)

A.D. 306–337	Constantine the Great.
313	So-called "Edict of Milan" frees the Christian religion.
c. 315	Pachomius founds first monastery.
325	Council of Nicaea: Arianism condemned.
330	Capital transferred to Byzantium, renamed Constantinople.
363–377	Persian power revives under Shapur II.
c. 370	Basil organizes eastern monachism.
	Barbarian pressure increases: Huns thrust Germans westward.
c. 375	Melania founds convent for women at Jerusalem.
378	Romans defeated at Adrianople: death of Valens.
380	Theodosius I makes Christianity official religion of empire.
386	Jerome settles in Bethlehem.
390	Thessalonica riot: Ambrose (bishop of Milan since 373) forces Theodosius to do penance.
391	Paganism finally proscribed.
396	Augustine chosen bishop of Hippo.
397	Death of Ambrose.
405	Radagaisus invades Italy.
406–409	Vandals, Alans, Suevi and Burgundians invade Gaul.
	Rome evacuates Britain: Angles, Saxons and Jutes invade it over next century.
408	Death of Stilicho.
410	Alaric sacks Rome.
c. 416	Visigoths in Aquitania.
420	Death of Jerome.
430	Vandals capture Hippo. Death of Augustine.
432	St Patrick in Ireland.
450	Marcian, first emperor to be crowned by Church.
451	Defeat of Attila near Troyes.
454	Death of Aëtius.
455	Gaiseric sacks Rome.
472	Ricimer takes Rome: death.
496	Baptism of Clovis.
529	St Benedict founds Monte Cassino.
536–546	Belisarius in Italy.
553	Ostrogoths finally crushed.
568	Lombards invade Italy.
597	Augustine of Canterbury lands.

INDEX